Caracas
VENEZUELA
Georgetown
Paramaribo
Cayenne
The GUIANAS
Brit
Dut
Fr
Bogotá
COLOMBIA
Quito
CUADOR
B R A Z I L
PERU
Lima
BOLIVIA
La Paz
Rio de Janeiro
PARAGUAY
Asunción
CHILE
ARGENTINA
URUGUAY
Santiago
Montevideo
Buenos Aires

FANTASTIC SOUTH AMERICA

FANTASTIC SOUTH

CONTINENT

AMERICA

OF THE FUTURE

HENRY LIONEL WILLIAMS

HORIZON PRESS NEW YORK

TO

Commander G. M. Dyott, guide, mentor, and friend in jungle days who showed me the real South America and the first South Americans

Library of Congress Catalog Card Number 58-10345
Printed in the United States of America

CONTENTS

Picture Credits

ARGENTINE AIRLINES: 4, 5, 29

BRAZILIAN GOVERNMENT TRADE BUREAU: 26, 27, 31, 34, 35

COMMANDER DYOTT: 28, 47, 50

CONSULATE GENERAL OF BOLIVIA: 24

CONSULATE GENERAL OF BRAZIL: 30, 33

CONSULATE GENERAL OF PARAGUAY: 14, 15, 16

GRACE LINE: 19, 20, 37, 39, 40, 51, 52, 53, 54, 56, 57, 58, 59

HAMILTON WRIGHT: 42, 44, 45, 46

MOORE MCCORMACK LINES: 6, 7, 8, 11, 12

PANAGRA: 2, 3, 18, 23, 36, 38, 49, 55

PEPSI-COLA INTERNATIONAL PANORAMA: 9, 48, 62

SOCONY MOBIL OIL CO., INC.: 43, 63, 64, 65

UNITED NATIONS: 1, 10, 13, 17, 21, 22, 25, 32, 60, 61, 66

H. L. WILLIAMS: 41

LIST OF ILLUSTRATIONS

INTRODUCTION

SOUTH AMERICA IS A LAND OF VIOLENT contrasts where Nature conspires to provide fantastic spectacles that emphasize the insignificance of Man. It is a land of four-mile-high mountains and vast, low-lying plains; of snow-capped peaks and steaming jungles, of glaciers, volcanoes and rainless deserts, a country of almost illimitable resources that Nature has made it difficult for man to exploit.

Similar contrasts prevail between the old and the new civilizations of the continent; between the ancient cultures that grew out of its soil, and the medieval European civilizations that were imposed upon them. They reveal the difficulties those early cultures had to face and the handicaps they had to overcome, isolated as they were from one another and the rest of the world. They give point to the decadence that has overtaken many of the subject peoples since they were conquered by the Spanish and the Portuguese, and the indifference with which their plight was long regarded by those who profited by their apathy and lack of ambition.

In South America today, jungle savages and the descendants of ancient cultures that flourished when Europe was inhabited by warring tribes are scattered over the seven million square miles of highland, lowland, seashore, and forest. Side by side with the more civilized aboriginals live the sons of their conquerors from the Iberian Peninsula four thousand miles away. For several hundred years these peoples have intermarried, and from them has sprung a race of South Americans possessing many of the finer attributes of each.

To understand their lives and the forces that have created them, it is necessary to understand the history and background of each of these interrelated civilizations, and the earth they occupy which has left its mark upon them.

On this southern continent, some 155 million people live in climates varying all the way from the eternal Spring of the high Andean plateaux to the sun-baked sands of the Pacific Coast and rain-drenched forests of the Amazon. From Cape Horn to the Caribbean, from the mouths of the Amazon to the Guayas Estuary, primitive tribal cultures have developed slowly over the centuries. In limited areas along the Andean ranges and coastal fringes, the Indo-Iberian nations, often diluted with Negro, English, Irish, German, and Italian blood have, for the most part, kept pace with the cultural and economic progress of comparable countries throughout the world, and in some cases outstripped them. Cultural traditions of antiquity and of medieval Europe have been kept alive by the great colleges, universities, libraries, and art museums of the South American Continent.

Thus, throughout the centuries, vast forces have been at work molding the lower continent which now seems destined to make even greater advances during the next twenty years than it has in the past hundred, despite the fact that the various nationalities and cultures still differ widely in their degree of civilization, economic level and political outlook.

The direction in which each of these nations is destined to develop depends upon many things, including the perception of its leaders. The course each takes will not be without its effects upon the others. In delving into these probabilities there are, of course, many questions to be answered. Probably the most obvious of such questions are those arising from comparisons with the North American Continent over which South America had a head start.

Why, for example, should our Continental United States support one-and-a-half times the population of South America with a land area less than half its size? Why should South America, occupying one seventh of the world's land area, support only one twenty-fourth of the world's people? And why are some of those countries which have a healthful climate, extensive natural resources, ample labor, and apparently everything necessary for the creation of a progressive and wealthy nation, not yet in a position to take their place among the leading powers of the world?

These are interesting and vital questions. Into them enter such basic factors as the character of the peoples, the level of their culture, the attitudes of the governments toward the original inhabitants and to immigrants; their political and social systems; their natural resources and their ability to develop them; their degree of agricultural, industrial, and commercial development, and the accessibility to the ports and markets of the world.

If we can find the answers to these things, and bring ourselves to understand the nature of these peoples and their capacities, we shall have a much clearer conception of their potentialities, and their possible future influence among the nations of the world.

The roads by which these various peoples have travelled to the places they have reached in world economy and cultural influence have depended upon many things. Beside the physical and psychological characteristics of the individuals concerned, we have to take into account the causes of their dispersal. We have to know how they came to live where they do, and the problems they are faced with as a result of living there. These include climate and natural resources, politics, wars and social disturbances, barriers to peaceful expansion such as belligerent neighbors, some of them savage; disease, and other natural enemies of mankind, and many other factors to be discussed in these pages, not forgetting the important item of Chance.

Speculation upon the vagaries of Chance may often prove fruitless but it is always interesting. In this instance, as we shall see, Chance lay behind the historic accidents which resulted in the settling of South America instead of North America by the Spaniards and Portuguese, and the division of the southern continent between them.

In the long drama, we shall see too how after centuries of uncertainty and experiment, of strife and turmoil, a point near stability has at last been reached by the advanced countries of our sister continent to the South.

The shadow of dictatorship, always diminishing with time, now moves only fitfully over ever smaller areas, and the vast continent is steadily moving into its rightful position as a unified force for good in a world beset by conflicting ideologies.

The growth of a democratic ideal has paralleled the growing realization that a creative future lies not in competition but in cooperation between the nations.

This book, then, is not simply the story of racial and cultural changes throughout the history of a continent. Rather it seeks to combine these things with other elements, human, natural and physical, in an exploration of the prime causes and motivations that have contributed to the development of the nations inhabiting South America and may foretell their place in the world of an imminent tomorrow.

—HENRY LIONEL WILLIAMS

JUNGLES, MEN AND MOUNTAINS

CHAPTER 1

JUNGLES, MEN AND MOUNTAINS

IT IS ALMOST FIVE HUNDRED YEARS since explorers from the fringe of Europe set out to prove that the world was round by sailing westward over the Atlantic. Beyond this mysterious Ocean Sea they hoped to find the Indies. Instead, they stumbled on the American continents which men from Asia had discovered and populated 20,000 years before.

When it became clear to the bewildered Europeans that this territory was not Far Cathay but a hitherto unknown land they proclaimed it the New World. They then proceeded to wrest portions of it from its original owners, just as the Anglo-Saxons were to do a hundred years later in the North.

A *Medieval Gold Rush*

Christopher Columbus, a navigator of uncertain national origin in the employ of Spain, was the first European explorer, so far as we know, to touch South America. That was in the Year of Grace 1498 when he sailed into one of the many mouths of the Orinoco River and sailed out again. The handful of pearls, the captive Indians, and the assortment of gold trinkets that he took back to Spain from this and other voyages started what turned out to be the medieval equivalent of a gold rush. This gold, however, was not to be secured by honest labor, but by murder and pillage which, in that more robust era, went under the name of lawful conquest.

It is not to be supposed from this that the Spaniards of this era were any worse in this respect than any of their contemporary European neighbors. Their attitude toward human life and suffering, we have to remember, was not as purely vicious as it may sound. They lived in times when the killing and maiming of people for simple crimes was an everyday occurrence even in the most enlightened countries. In many lands thieves had their hands chopped off; those who did not accept the prescribed religion were hanged, burned, or beheaded; the tongues of traitors were cut out; torture was part of the criminal code in the leading civilizations. More than two hundred years later we burned our "witches" in New England!

Furthermore, there was a great deal of suffering from accidents and other natural causes that there was no anesthetic to assuage. The cauterizing of wounds with hot oil or pitch, and the amputation of limbs without even a crack on the head to numb the senses were ordinary hazards that people learned to face throughout their lives. The story is told of Alonso de Ojeda, one of the early Spanish adventurers who, when wounded by a poisoned arrow, demanded that a red-hot iron be plunged into the wound. When the physician protested, Ojeda threatened to kill himself if he was refused. Such men apparently could endure as much as they inflicted on others, though, of course, according to our modern code, that is no excuse at all.

In those days, as occasionally in more recent times, all people of foreign lands, particularly those whose skin or language were different, or who worshipped unconventional gods, were looked upon as barbarians, regardless of their level of culture. They were automatically classed as infidels and outcasts, doomed to perdition, and their subjection or extermination were laudable objectives of which all civilized people heartily approved. Thus it was that in the first few years of the Sixteenth Century, Spanish adventurers set out to acquire sudden riches from the "ignorant savages" of South America with the blessings of their rulers and the Holy Roman Church.

Pizarro and the Incas

If there had been no advanced civilization in the lower continent when the Spanish came, the history of modern South America would have been far different from what it turned out to be. What happened when that lusty Spanish adventurer, Francisco Pizarro, and his accomplices got wind of the Inca gold should, of course, be no occasion for surprise. The same thing might well have happened in North America if the first explorers had found it occupied by barbarians who did not know that the gold they displayed and used so lavishly was to the invading white man a metal more precious than life itself. This was the reason that the serious conquest of the southern continent started on the western coast where the empire of the Incas lay.

Only the enthusiasm of the Spanish *conquistadores* for the excitement—and profit—of treasure hunting led them to explore the rest of the country at all.

The lack of gold-plated, emerald-studded temples on the Atlantic side of the Continent was largely responsible for its early neglect by both Spaniards and Portuguese. Only the inquisitive interest of other nations finally forced Portugal into taking steps to stake out and protect her claim. From such sordid and ignoble beginnings grew the splendid Iberian empires that within the last hundred and thirty years or so have expanded into the ten Republics that occupy nearly all of South America today.

The original inhabitants of the southern continent, as it turned out, were not to be exterminated as their brothers in the North were later. There was too great a need for the labor of the more civilized natives; and the rest, who dwelt in the jungles, were of little interest to the invaders because they had nothing of value of which they could be robbed. As a result, except for a few more belligerent tribes who had to be suppressed, conquerors and conquered existed side by side for the next four hundred years during which time their relationships changed completely. Through intermarriage, concubinage, and other forms of miscegenation, a new hybrid people developed, possessing for the most part the finer attributes of both the Iberians and the South American Indians.

Naturally, the pure-blooded Spaniards considered themselves far superior to the Indians and to those of mixed blood *(mestizos)*. Nevertheless, the mixing went on, and both Indians and mestizos gradually came to occupy important positions in the life of the various nations.

Today, the Ibero-Indians (mestizos) form a large section of the South American population. There are also great numbers of other races who have had considerable effect on the social, political, and economic developments within the ten Latin-American nations. Nevertheless these developments, in the main, are largely the result of the character and the background of the original inhabitants of the Continent, their environment, and their fusion with other races and cultures during the past four hundred years. They and the Spanish and Portuguese are the basic stocks from which today's inhabitants of South America have sprung, and the so-called Indians who have some Spanish blood still form the largest proportion of the Continent's people although they do not predominate in every country.

In order to understand the influence that the continent's original inhabitants have had on the character of their modern descendants, and on the development of their respective countries, it is necessary to go back to the time of the invasion and to see who and what these people were, where they came from, and what the places they lived in were like, and also the effects upon them of their surroundings and conditions.

The Face of a Continent

South America, being a large continent, contains many kinds of country and has a variety of climates. No one knows for certain just how many people lived in South America at the time of the Conquest. It is estimated that there could well have been twenty-five to thirty millions scattered throughout its seven million square miles, which means that there was plenty of room for everyone even though ten to twenty millions of people may have been concentrated in the Andean highlands and the Western coastal strip.

It was, however, not the area of land so much as its vertical structure—its mountains, plains, and plateaux—that determined its possibilities for human habitation and exploitation. Since most of the country is in the tropical zone, altitude has always had an important effect on the climate. While the area at the foot of a mountain might be constantly scorched by the tropical sun, a high valley in the heart of the mountains might well have a cool and equable climate the year round. This actually happens in the region of the high mountains of South America where modern cities flourish two miles above the sea. Even the less elevated plains and tablelands are far more suited to the development of the more progressive cultures than the oppressive heat and humidity of the wooded lowlands. South America fortunately has vast areas of almost every conceivable kind of terrain.

The most striking and important physical feature of South America is the great mountain chain of the Andes. This wall of snow-thatched peaks forms a colossal bulwark along the entire west coast from Tierra del Fuego to the Caribbean. For 4,400 miles, these sky-rending giants hug the coast line, leaving between their foothills and the Pacific Ocean a plain that varies in width from twenty to one hundred miles.

From northern Chile to the Guayas Estuary in Ecuador—a distance of almost two thousand miles—this plain is dry and sandy, except for occasional ribbons of green that betray the presence of lost rivers that have vanished on their way to the sea, and neither plants nor reptiles can live upon it. This is one place in the world where raindrops can be said to be "scarcer than ice cubes in Hades!" North of the Guayas the coast is smothered in tropical growth. These phenomena are due less to the mountains than to the vagaries of an ocean current, the Humboldt, of which we shall have more to say later.

The gigantic mountain ranges of the Andes are one hundred to four hundred miles across. They not only affect, and often prohibit, access from the west coast to the vast expanse of territory on the east, but determine the climate of both to a very large degree.

The northeast and southeast trade winds sweep in from the Atlantic over the eastern coast of the Continent. Converging on the hot and humid doldrums, almost along the equator, the winds rise, and becoming cool, lose the moisture they have picked up over the ocean. This moisture is precipitated in the form of torrential rains. Much of the rain falls upon the eastern flanks of the Andes. It rushes down to the tree-covered plains in myriad streams that finally join to form the Amazon, the world's largest river. The resulting high humidity and the tropical heat—a combination deadly to humans—fill the Amazon Valley from the Andes to the Atlantic with dense vegetation of all kinds that teems with insect and animal life.

In prehistoric days, it is supposed, the Amazon Valley and the adjacent lowlands, extending northward to the Orinoco River and south to the River Plate (La Plata) may have been the bottom of an inland sea. They give every evidence of it, being extremely flat and almost at zero altitude. Even today, in the wet season, the Amazon overflows its almost non-existent banks and floods the jungles for miles around. The lowlands, where winding rivers form the only trails through the dense forests, extend from the Andes to the plateaux of Guiana and the tablelands of Brazil.

The Guiana plateaux stretch eastward from the Orinoco toward the mouths of the Amazon. The great tablelands of Brazil and the higher ridges that surmount them (remnants of mountains that probably were once higher than the Andes) follow the eastern coast, rising in many places right out of the sea. At their southern end, these plateaux melt into thousand-mile-long, almost treeless, grassy plains, the pampas of Argentina. In the north the lowlands constitute the *llanos*, or prairies, of Venezuela. For the most part these are dry as a desert in summer, but in the wet seasons they are deep in grass.

This, then, is South America from the standpoint of its major physical features—a vast area, largely tropical, divided into many contrasting zones. The western coastal strip is mostly arid and hot; the west Andean slopes are for the most part dry and steep. The foothills of the Andes, the moderately high plateaux and the interandine valleys have temperate climates and profuse vegetation. On the still higher plateaux where the air is thin and cold few food crops can be grown. The eastern slope of the Andes, which is washed by heavy rains, becomes progressively more warm and humid as the altitude decreases. At the bottom of these slopes lie the rain jungles of the lowlands occupying an area as large as the Continent of Australia. Beyond them are the pleasantly habitable highlands of the eastern seaboard.

In the dark and dank rain forests of the Amazon basin few humans have ever lived at all. Crocodiles, monkeys, bats, birds, and bloodsucking insects are everywhere. The trees are large and clothed in parasitic growths and hanging vines that twist and loop like hangman's nooses. The trunks of the trees are hidden by dense leafage which shuts out most of the light filtering through the steam clouds that form after every shower.

The constant heat and damp are kind to the gaudy orchids that decorate the trees, but they combine to make the air too oppressive for human existence. The only trails through these grassless morasses and swamps are the rivers, most of which are shallow when they are not inundating the floor of the jungle. The numerous sandbanks form comfortable snoozing grounds for the crocodiles and convenient hiding places for their eggs.

The more primitive humans have long occupied the highlands of the east and the llanos and *selvas* (forests) of the north, where at least there is some relief from the heat and damp. The comparatively civilized peoples, whose riches tempted the avaricious invaders, lived in the foothills west of the Andean ranges in the wide central part of the coastal plain and in the Andean highlands.

The Aboriginals/The First Americans and their Origins

So much for the terrain; now let us look at the Indians themselves. Few peoples in all history have aroused more speculation as to their origin than the aboriginals of South America. For decades archaeologists and anthropologists have argued and contended, and even today there is no great unanimity of opinion among them. Nevertheless, out of all this welter of controversy which, incidentally, involves the whole of the Americas, certain facts emerge that are fairly well substantiated.

Apparently about twenty thousand years ago a wave of emigration to the American continents started from some remote spot in Asia. This was at the end of the last Ice Age. Probably, as the ice retreated, the animals that the ancients hunted moved north to fresh pastures. The hunters followed, and so found themselves in the territory we now call Siberia, looking across the water to the distant shores of a new and tempting land. At any rate this human tide, which probably flowed for thousands of years, passed over the Bering Straits, which may then have been more or less continually solid ice and probably much narrower. Reaching the mainland of America a great many paths were open to them.

Some of these roving people settled in Alaska and North America generally, but large numbers of them drifted down the western coast, through the narrow neck of Central America, and so found themselves at the gateway of a wide and unknown world.

Like the later European arrivals on the American Continent, in all probability these early migrants had no remote idea where they were or what lay before them. It seems certain that they could not have been far advanced culturally and that they lived in an archaic state. They had no knowledge of the wheel and and no idea of the domestication of animals, although they brought the dog with them. They had no written language nor any system of records. They were, at first, true Stone Age people of the most primitive type whose greatest achievements eventually were the use of bows, spear throwers, and the fire-drill.

Possibly the infiltration into South America was slow. First the migrant peoples may have settled farther north, only gradually moving on to new hunting grounds as necessity dictated. On the other hand they may have been late arrivals on the American Continents, forced to travel south in search of space not already pre-empted by earlier settlers. In any case, as most authorities agree, none of these peoples was a part or offshoot of any higher civilization that had taken root and developed farther north.

Since the influx was spread over so long a period, of course it is quite possible that later arivals may have been of a more advanced type. We do know that from very early times the higher cultures made pottery, domesticated animals, and raised cotton. Cotton, together with the wool of alpacas and wild vicuñas, and the brilliant feathers of birds were used to make garments and decorative articles.

Regardless of their relative cultural achievements, all of the newcomers to South America were faced with the same decision—whether to plunge inland along the jungle-filled valleys and rivers, to make for the hills, or to keep to the sea shore. What guided them in their decisions we shall never know. Some of them found their way along the Caribbean coast; some clung to the Pacific, others followed the valleys or climbed over the mountains into the Amazon vale. Still more of them drifted along the highlands. And so, little by little, century after century, these early settlers spread their habitations over the Continent, from Panama to Patagonia, each group or culture selecting the terrain that suited it best. Many of them, however, did not abandon their nomadic life, and others were forced by circumstances and hostile neighbors to seek territories less desirable but more safe.

Most of the available evidence suggests that it was in

this manner that Man came to South America, although the islands of the West Indies may have furnished stepping-stones for some of them. From the beginning there were many things to check their progress in addition to the hazards of the terrain. There were, it is true, no particularly large and ferocious animals to bar their path or to prey upon them once they had set up their habitations. But doubtless the insects and parasites and the diseases they bred, as well as the reptiles and the small, flesh-eating fishes (the *caribes* or *piranhas*) took their toll.

Now although these people came to the south continent in a slow and often broken stream they all had the same basic characteristics. This we can tell from the present-day individuals who are their descendants. They were all brown-skinned (although some were lighter in complexion than others), black-haired with brown eyes . . . all typically and unmistakably what we call Indians, both in appearance and psychological traits. In origin they were undoubtedly Asiatic, of what the anthropologists call the proto-Mongoloid type.

Most visitors to South America have noted examples of the Mongol characteristics—the combination of prominent cheek bones and slightly "slanted" eyes, an illusion produced by the overlapping corners of the eyelids called the Mongoloid fold. But this does not mean that the Indians are Mongols or of Mongol descent; they are not brothers to the yellow-skinned races of the East. All that this proto-Mongoloid business means is that these Indians are descended from the same root stock as the Mongols, just as Man himself is believed by scientists to have descended from the same root stock as the higher apes. They are not close relatives, but divergent types stemming from the same original source.

Terrain, Climate and Culture

These archaic peoples, then, were the raw materials which were to develop over a period of some thousands of years into the comparatively modern Indian tribes and cultures that the European explorers found. In that long period many changes had taken place. The individuals and the groups had had to adjust themselves to their environment and, in turn, their habitat had influenced their way of life, their thought, and their needs.

Throughout the history of the world mankind appears to have fared best in comparatively temperate climates and the physical and geographical conditions that go with them. Next favorable to the development of civilizations come the semi-tropical climates and the tropical regions outside the forests. This tendency seems to have prevailed in the case of South America where the various cultures have developed almost side by side under widely differing climatic and geographical conditions, and with varying results.

Along the fringes of the more open Amazon forests where the damp and heat are more suited to plant life than to human existence, the Indians remained for the most part nomadic savages, building no permanent shelters. They lived by hunting and fishing, and made little cultural progress. Higher in the hills, on the eastern slopes of the mountains and the highlands of the east the Indians developed to a point where they founded small settlements or villages such as they have today.

Some of the tribes, like the Shuaros, of which the head-shrinking Jívaros are a part, built large family huts, scattered throughout the jungle and usually near a river. Such houses would be shared by three generations of a family, with the oldest male as their head, or chief. In other Indian cultures the village was the central unit, made up of individual or family-group houses. Such cultures developed better weapons and better group-hunting methods. From them, for instance, came the blowpipe and poisoned darts, the communal fishing expeditions in which drugs were used to paralyze the fish as they swam, with huge basket nets stretched across the river to catch them in.

In the higher altitudes where the terrain is more open a different type of communal existence evolved in which agriculture played a large part. The haphazard growing of yucca (cassava, manioc, or mandioca) and plantains gave way to the more careful cultivation of plants, more skilled storage and preparation of garden products. Maize and sometimes tobacco were added to the short list of things grown, though potatoes, which originated in Peru, were reserved to the still more advanced cultural groups of the higher plateaux and the mountain sides.

And so, when the Spaniards and Portuguese first set foot on South American soil they found it occupied by a variety of cultures ranging from the primitive jungle tribes to the flourishing empire of the Incas. In the north they came in contact with the cannibalistic Caribs and the more friendly and fastidious boat-building Arawaks.

Farther inland were the comparatively civilized Chibchas who made great stone images and ornaments of gold and emeralds. In the southeast lived a conglomeration of tribes called the Tupi-Guaranis, and in the southwest the fierce and independent Araucanians who remain unconquered to this day. On the western flanks of the Andes the empire of the Incas extended from Lake Titicaca in the south to Quito in the north.

No one knows much of the history of these peoples with the exception of the Incas, whose predecessors seem to have possessed an even higher civilization, and of those of some of their subject peoples. It is an interesting point as to whether the higher cultures developed first and then sought out the kind of terrain adapted to their needs and ways of living, or whether their original choice of a place to live was responsible for their more rapid advance in culture. In most cases the evidence would suggest that location was a matter of deliberate choice, although the choice may have been made for reasons quite foreign to those which produced the most important benefits.

These earlier arrivals, it must be remembered, were of necessity nomads. That was the reason they left their homes in Asia and travelled many thousands of miles in pursuit of the necessities of life. There was nothing to keep them in any one place, and they were forever seeking territory in which the animals they hunted were more plentiful and easier to obtain. They were essentially meat-eaters and rarely stayed in one place long enough to cultivate vegetable foods.

Intertribal Commerce

The one thing these archaic peoples did find almost everywhere on the American continents was *cassava.* To them this was probably the staff of life, when once they had learned to distinguish betwen the poisonous and non-poisonous varieties, and how to get rid of the poison by grinding and squeezing out the juice. This edible root was their bread, and from it they soon learned how to make an intoxicating drink. Cassava was easy to grow and it grew quickly. All that was needed to be done was to stick a branch in the ground and Nature would do the rest. These first arrivals, however, must have found cassava in its wild state. The plant made it possible for them to live in places where otherwise they would have been unable to exist.

As their hunting methods and weapons improved, and they were able to add fish and berries, and other roots to their menus, these nomads were able to stay longer in one place. They did not need so large an area to hunt over and so did not come into conflict with other tribes bent on the same mission. Settled in one spot for a considerable period, they were able to concentrate on ways of improving their living conditions. They were able to give more attention to the structure and facilities of their houses. Groups of them banded together for mutual protection, and the restrictions this imposed upon them formed the foundation of tribal law. Out of this also grew the interchange of products and the beginnings of specialization. Many jungle tribes, for example, settled in places where there was an abundance of clay for making pottery. Others stripped bark off trees to make *tapa* cloth; still others discovered deposits of salt, and so inter-tribal commerce was developed.

Importance of the Early Civilizations

The more intelligent people naturally gave thought to their needs and left less to chance. They searched for what they needed and so progressed faster than those of lesser ambition and those handicapped by fears and superstitions. In this way the better cultures sought out places to live in which Nature placed fewer handicaps on their existence and growth. And, in South America they had plenty of choice.

Just how far such primitive cultures could develop in the course of a few thousand years is well demonstrated by the rise of the Araucanians, the Chibchas, and the Incas, and the peoples from whom they sprang or whom they absorbed. It is instructive to consider these higher cultures in some detail not only because of the influence they have had on the history of modern South America, but also because of the important lesson we can draw from their achievements in studying the present-day brown-skinned folk who have made a vital contribution to the South American economy, and whose intermarriage with the white men has produced an admirable race of people, the South American mestizos (in Brazil: mamelucos).

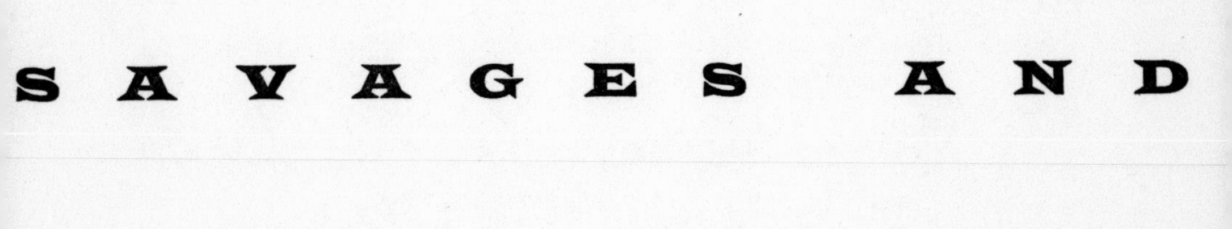

CIVILIZATION

CHAPTER 2 SAVAGES AND CIVILIZATION

THE ORIGIN OF THE INCAS IS WRAPPED in mystery. They began to form their empire early in the twelfth century, but it is very certain that no civilization such as theirs could have been developed between that date and the arrival of the Spaniards four hundred years later. Mankind does not progress that fast. What the Incas did do in that time, however, was to bring a large number of tribes and smaller cultures under their rule, welding them into a strong and unified empire. As a matter of fact, life under the Incas was so attractive to Indians of lesser cultures that some of them voluntarily asked to be taken into the confederation.

The Inca World/The Tiahuanacos

The Inca system was thoroughly socialistic, even communistic in some respects, and the individual did not have much personl liberty. For the less civilized Indians, who seem to have found any kind of existence a struggle, the system which provided them with work and land and assured them of security throughout their lifetime, left little to be desired.

There are many legends connected with the coming of the Incas, but the only known facts are that before they sowed the seeds of the empire in the city of Cuzco their forebears had built up an advanced civilization in the Lake Titicaca region of the Bolivian Andes. The predecessors of these people were probably the Tiahuanacos, who built fortresses and temples of shaped stones weighing many tons. These stones, some of them 30 feet long and 5 feet thick, were so carefully fitted together without mortar that even to this day a knife blade cannot be inserted in the joints. They also carved huge figures and cut an entire gateway out of a single piece of stone. Some of the stones they decorated with elaborate carving. All this bespeaks manual skills and artistic development of a high order.

At a late period, these Tiahuanacos came down from their mountains to subdue or absorb the people of the lowlands with whom they had traded for centuries. It was probably they who built much of Cuzco which was to become the capital of the Incan empire long after the Tiahuanaco civilization had vanished from the sight of men.

The Incas occupied territory that is now a part of seven countries—Argentina, Bolivia, Chile, Peru, Colombia, and Brazil—an area about 1,200 miles long and almost 500 miles wide. Their empire included several cultures that formerly had had fairly well-developed civilizations of their own. In northern Peru, for example, were the Chimus. Their great capital city of Chan-Chan, the ruins of which can be seen today, stretched for miles over the dry coastal plain. So far advanced were the Chimus that they had constructed huge reservoirs and aqueducts, part of an intensive irrigation system that turned the desert into a garden.

Inside a 50-foot-high wall of adobe stood a palace of 500 rooms, the interior walls of which, so it is believed, were covered with gold leaf. There were also temples, granaries, and many small houses of stone with reed roofs. The Chimus made the most beautiful pottery that has ever been found on the American continents—a great deal of it in the form of portrait ware. It is the pictorial decoration of this pottery that has enabled us to reconstruct a fairly accurate picture of the life of these people before they were swallowed up in the spreading Inca tide. They also wove exquisite cotton materials and feather work, as well as tapestries that are more than the equal of any produced in Europe in the Middle Ages.

Since the Chimus for their water supply depended on streams running down from the mountains to the ocean, it was necessary to protect the sources of those streams so that no enemy could dam or divert the water and so make resistance futile. These people therefore built a tremendous wall, connecting a series of forts, high into the mountains. But even this did not prevent the Incas from besieging Chan-Chan and taking the city by shutting off the water supply, just a hundred years before the Spaniards came.

At the other end of Peru, which occupied a great deal more territory than it does now, there was the advanced civilization of the Nazcas. They too were highly artistic in their pottery and tapestry designs. But where the Chimus' pottery was realistic, most of the Nazca ware was symbolic and the designs highly conventionalized.

The extent of the Nazca territory seems to have been limited to four adjacent valleys running down to the coast. Both the Chimus and the Nazcas were people of the lowlands. The Tiahuanacos originally occupied the highlands, but by the time the Incas came on the scene this great culture had vanished. Only the magnificent ruins of its forts and temples remained.

The first Incas appeared somewhere south of Cuzco, a town with an elevation of 11,500 feet. Lake Titicaca, southeast of Cuzco, on the shores of which the Tiahuanacos dwelt, is 1,000 feet higher in the mountains, and covers an area of 5,500 square miles. Although the Tiahuanacos eventually expanded their territory as far as the coast, the available evidence indicates that there were several very advanced cultures in this area long before the Incas took over.

The Incas, themselves, who were originally a small ruling group, seem to have specialized in government. They gradually extended their control over the peoples of the highlands and lowlands, and encouraged the development of agriculture and husbandry as well as the arts. They also built up a large and well-equipped army, both to maintain internal peace and to resist invasion.

A long period of consolidation followed the acquisition of each new piece of territory. This gave the arts of peace a chance to develop and the country was not impoverished by constant wars. Therefore the people had a chance to progress culturally and excel their neighbors in the useful arts, while becoming even more united among themselves through equality under the law and the security that a paternal government provided.

Their leader was known as the Inca, and the rule

descended to the first son by his chief wife. It was customary for each new Inca to make personal tours of inspection of his entire domain. In this way the people had the opportunity to see their ruler, and he became to them much more of a reality and less of an abstract idea. Although he was considered divine, being a descendant of the Sun God, they learned that he had human qualities and was not unapproachable. The Inca and the nobles were careful to foster this idea by actually taking part in the cultivation of land during certain ceremonial periods.

The travels of the Incas and the needs of the army led to the construction of roads to all parts of the empire, with rest houses and supply stations at regular intervals along the way. In developing these roads they made use of highways constructed by the Tiahuanacos for the purpose of trading with the people of the lowlands. Rivers and ravines were crossed by wooden or stone bridges, or by suspension bridges made of vines or fiber cables, some of the cables being almost a foot thick. By means of couriers located at stations every few miles along the roads, messages could be sent from one end of the empire to the other, a distance of 1,200 miles, in ten days.

Arts of the Incas

In the 400 years of their recorded existence the Incas developed their arts and crafts to a high degree, and were never above learning from the peoples they conquered and absorbed. Strangely enough, they never invented the wheel or made uses of devices incorporating that principle. Their building methods improved through the lessons they learned from the Tiahuanaco ruins, but their greatest advance probably lay in the intensive agricultural system they developed. In this rugged country where hot suns alternated with torrential rains, the hillsides were terraced from top to bottom to provide level planting areas that could not be washed away. Where irrigation was necessary, water was brought from greater altitudes by stone conduits and ditches.

Perhaps an even better measure of the cultural achievements of these people lies in the development of their minor arts. Gold and silver were used in enormous quantities for the making of exquisitely designed vessels, decorative pieces, and religious objects. Their tapestries and brocades, mostly decorated with geometric figures, have never been excelled either in color or design. However, their art did not end there. They also excelled in music, poetry, and the drama, though writing was unknown. Plays were performed both in the palaces of the rulers and in the villages of their subjects.

The medical arts had been developed to a high degree, and surgery was practiced with astonishing success. Not only were bones set, but pieces of the skull were removed without killing the patient, and exposed parts of the brain were covered with silver plates. Medicines consisted of herbs or the juices of plants. Cocaine in the form of coca leaves was used as a narcotic, and quinine for the reduction of fevers. It is unfortunate that the Spanish conquerors encouraged the chewing of coca leaves by the peons. This quickly became a national habit that enslaved the Indian from that time on. The importance of this in future developments will be discussed in due course.

At its zenith, the Inca empire controlled the destinies

of around twenty million persons, each one of whom had his duties and obligations to the state carefully defined. Until they were sixteen years old children had no duties. From sixteen to twenty they did light manual labor, and for the next five years either became apprenticed to a trade or worked with their elders in the fields. At twenty-five a youth became a man, was required to marry, and to pay tribute from the products of the land that was given him to work. He continued as head of the household from then on. But at fifty he was considered "half old" and was only required to do light work for the next ten years. After sixty the state supported him in comfort.

Each man was given about five acres of land for the support of himself and his wife, and extra land for each child. From the produce of that land, one third was kept for the family, and one third went to the government, and one third to the Inca. That portion allotted to the Inca was stored in the political division of the country from which it originated, and was used for the common good. It formed insurance against poor crops and provided for the support of the old and indigent. The government share supported the public servants, officers of the state, and the priests. Craftsmen operated along similar lines, though they had no land. They contributed workmanship, and the materials they used were provided by the state.

Members of the hereditary ruling class lived no simple life of ease. The young people underwent rigorous training in subjects such as history, theology, law, and mathematics, which would fit them for their future positions. They were also put through a period of stringent physical training.

Those who worked the land did not own it and could not sell it or otherwise dispose of it. Everything belonged to the state, except the individual's household goods, utensils, tools, clothing, their dogs, and the small animals, such as guineapigs, that they raised for food. Since there was no money, all these things were acquired by barter.

The best testimony to the success of this system that we have is the fact that the people rarely rebelled, and lying and thievery were reputedly unknown. This is not surprising, since no one was required to do more than he was easily capable of doing; the laws were not oppressive but logical and fair, and they applied equally to everyone from the Inca on down. The success of the Incas was undoubtedly due in large measure to the fact that they recognized the importance of the individual and the need for keeping him contented with his lot, as well as maintaining his faith in the justice of the State.

Of all the other Indian cultures in South America at the time of the conquest, by far the most advanced were those of the Chibchas and the Araucanians. Unfortunately for posterity, the Chibchas, whose territory extended from Panama through central Colombia almost to Ecuador, were practically annihilated within a few years after the Spaniards arrived.

The Legend of El Dorado

The capital city of the Chibchas lay on a forty-mile-long plateau—one of a series of *sabanas* that extend 200 miles along the eastern *cordillera* of the Andes—at an elevation of 8,600 feet. It occupied the site of the present city of Bogotá, the capital of Colombia. The Chibcha government was headed by two rulers, or *caciques,* and a spiritual leader, to whom historians refer as the High Priest. The Chibchas' vast territory was divided into two districts, each governed by one of the caciques. It was one of these men, the cacique of Guatavita, whose activities gave rise to the legend of El Dorado.

The story was that during an annual religious ceremony, this chief had his body covered with powdered gold. Taken on a raft to the middle of a sacred lake, he plunged into the water so that the gold was washed off. Meanwhile, the excited populace threw ornaments and objects of gold into the lake to add to the treasure thus offered to their gods. Probably the whole story was an elaborate hoax perpetrated by Indians, some of whom have a far greater sense of humor than is generally suspected. At any rate, the legend was responsible in no small degree for the practical extermination of these colorful and highly intelligent people, by the gold-mad invaders.

The Chibchas' was an agricultural civilization, their chief cereal crop being maize which they cultivated on an enormous scale. They also mined copper and emeralds, and dug salt from a mine that is still in operation. They wove and dyed fine cloth, and made exquisite ornaments of gold. Their pottery was richly decorated, made in the form of figurines and whistles, as well as shaped into the more conventional utensils. They sculptured stone images, built magnificent temples and—what is more astonishing—developed a system of weights and measures.

The Araucanians were much less advanced in their civilization than the Chibchas or the Incas. They were semi-nomadic, meat-eating herdsmen, with a strong system of government and an intense feeling of nationalism. A physically powerful and virile race, with skins of a light yellowish brown, they prized their independence above all else, and fought so desperately to retain their liberty that they were never conquered. The Incas forced them a considerable distance southward, but in the end abandoned all thought of conquering or absorbing them. For 200 years the Spaniards tried to subdue them, and finally were forced to acknowledge them as an independent nation. This they remain to this day, though the territory they live in has been part of Chile for over three quarters of a century.

Caribs, Arawaks, The Tupi Language Group

Throughout the rest of the continent the aboriginals were mostly savages, as some of them still are. It is not an easy matter to indicate the areas occupied by the various tribes and cultures, since they take no stock of political boundaries nor are they isolated in specific groups. The Caribs, for instance, are found all over the West Indies, throughout Venezuela and in small pockets in Brazil. Similarly, the Arawaks are scattered over Colombia, Venezuela, the Guianas, western Brazil, and even Peru! The Tupi language group clings to the coast of Brazil and the Amazon basin, part of Argentina and Bolivia.

Belonging to this group were the Guaranís, who played an important part in the settling of the areas which later formed Paraguay and Argentina, and were responsible for the Spanish invasion of Peru from the east coast. These tribes were much more advanced than the Indians along the western borders of Brazil, the Chaco Boreal, and the western banks of the rivers Paraná and Plata. As a rule, they were friendly toward the Spaniards, co-operating with them on several occasions. The capital of their confederation was a place called Lambaré where the Guaranís had a temple dedicated to the worship of a serpent god. Their weapons were the bow and the spear. Both men and women wore ornaments of silver which they procured by barter from the Caracaras, an Indian tribe on the Bolivian plateau under Inca domination. The Guaranís, while peaceably inclined for the most part, were a fierce and determined lot in warfare, and apparently had many battles with the Pampa Indians. The weapons of these Indians included the *boleadoras*—two or three stone balls attached to rawhide thongs which, when thrown, tangled the legs of beast or man and brought them down—weapons they were to use later with great effect against the Spaniards mounted on horseback.

These peoples, then, with the Araucanians and Chibchas, plus the Inca groups of the Ayamarás and Quechuas, formed the predominant cultures. The rest of the continent was occupied by about seventy smaller cultural units. While all of the more backward cultures differed in various respects—some being fierce and warlike, others fairly peaceable and friendly toward strangers—they had little to offer the Europeans and did not even make good slaves. Most of them were pretty much on a level culturally, and had many of the same physical and psychological traits. On the other hand, there were tribes, such as the Botocudos in Brazil, who were extremely primitive. The Botocudos were entirely nomadic, living on game which they ate in an uncleaned, half-burnt condition, like animals, as well as on fruit. The rest were, for the most part, at the Stone Age level of culture in the year 1500, and such minor variations as polygamy were more a result of necessity than specific tribal custom. At the other end of the scale were the well-organized tribes like the Arawaks who built substantial huts, made pottery, wove cloth, and cultivated a number of vegetables. They also made themselves excellent canoes with which to fish or to hunt game along the forest streams or ocean shores.

These, then, were the original occupants of the continent of South America. Their varied contributions to the progress of the individual nations throughout the past 400 years have had no small influence on their history and may determine their future position in world affairs. What that position is likely to be we can best judge from a brief survey of the events leading up to the present-day relationships between the races, their mutual attitudes and aspirations.

CONQUISTADORS

IN THE MAKING

CHAPTER 3

CONQUISTADORS IN THE MAKING

ONE OF THE MOST REMARKABLE MILITARY achievements of all time was undoubtedly the conquest of South America by a handful of Spaniards and still fewer Portuguese. These few hundred adventurers from Europe began their subjugation of the continent a century before the first British colonists landed on the North American coast. In short order they had possessed themselves, in the name of God and King, of an area more than thirty times as large as Spain and Portugal combined.

Considering the conditions they faced in their explorations, the smallness of their ships, the meagerness of their finances and supplies, and the insignificant number who took part in this fantastic gamble, the achievement was little short of miraculous.

The Mad Hunt for Gold

Regardless of what we may think of the motives of these men, and however far from admirable their methods, we have to admit that their courage was beyond question, even in an age when (we like to think) life was cheaper and men more cruel. From the outset these swashbuckling adventurers made their purpose clear. They did not come to found a new nation nor to establish colonies; they did not seek to escape persecution, nor even to develop the natural resources of this new-found world. Their purpose was plunder. The lure that drew them on, and for which they faced incredible hardships and inflicted untold misery, was gold. Each man sought only riches for himself; that was the sole object for which he was prepared to endure and, if necessary, die. The glory of the homeland and the salvation of heathen souls were complicating accompaniments the conquistadors were forced to promote to ensure the continued favor of their rulers and the often too-enthusiastic cooperation of the Church.

With them, bloodletting and slaughter were insignificant trifles incidental to the achievement of their major object in life—the accumulation of wealth by force of arms. And this was not merely a characteristic of the few, the renegades and scamps, the murderous fringe of a highly respectable civilization. This was the normal attitude of the more intelligent and better educated, footloose men of the twin nations that had for 1600 years writhed under the heel of one conqueror after another; men who had absorbed the aggressive, violent intensity and hardness of the warrior invaders whose blood, mixed with that of their aboriginal forebears, flowed in their veins.

It was, in truth, the nature of the people themselves, the product of their historic background, combined with their peculiar geographic situation in the ancient world, that was responsible for their eager acceptance of every opportunity for the acquisition of riches by conquest instead of by trade.

Perhaps no other nation of the world had developed from more mixed stock than these inhabitants of the Iberian Peninsula, the Spanish and Portuguese. In the veins of many of them flowed the blood of Phoenicians, Greeks, Celts, Romans, Vandals, Alans, Suevis, Visigoths, Moslems, Jews, all imposed upon that of the original Iberian tribes. Their way of life, their attitude of intolerance, their intense religious zeal, their disdain of labor and the glorification of battle, all were characteristics directly traceable to their historical experiences and development. These were the characteristics that enabled them to undertake the conquest of a vast, unknown territory for personal aggrandizement and, secondarily (by way of insurance for their souls), for the glory of the Church. These were the qualities that they brought to the building of mighty empires in the western world, and the legacy they left their descendants in the modern republics that we know today.

Iberian Origins

The roots of all this go back to about 1100 B.C. when there was no Spain or Portugal, only a broad and inviting peninsula at the gateway between the Atlantic and the Mediterranean Sea—a rugged country populated by scattered tribes called Iberians from whom the peninsula takes its name.

The Iberian Peninsula suffered throughout its history from the fact that it formed a natural highway between Africa and Europe. It is virtually in the same latitudes as the U.S.A., and has almost as wide a variety of climates. The climate and geography must have had no little to do with the shaping of the temperament of its people. The peninsula has its high, snow-capped mountains, semi-tropical lowlands, a scattering of bleak plateaux, and western and southern coastal plains that slope gently to the sea.

A wide variation in temperatures accompanies this diversity of altitudes, but nowhere are those temperatures extreme. In no inhabited region does it ever go much below freezing point, and in the summers temperatures average around 68 degrees. Nevertheless, while some sections are fertile, a great deal of the country is a dry and unproductive wilderness.

Of historic importance also is the unevenness of the rainfall and the infertility of much of the soil. In the northwest it rains too much—the precipitation ranges from fifty to seventy inches a year. Along the west coast and in the southwest, the total annual rainfall varies between twenty and fifty inches. This is sufficient for all normal purposes, provided it falls at the proper seasons and not all at once. Between five and ten inches is all that the south and southeast sections get, which is too little for the proper cultivation of agricultural and vinicultural crops. Along the Mediterranean coast even this small amount of rain comes too late in the year to be of much benefit. As a consequence, the farmers and vineyardists have to resort to artificial irrigation of the soil.

To sum up, the climate in medieval days, it seems from this distance, was either subtropical enough to make men lazy, or too dry or too wet to bring good results with little labor. This, added to the natural, easygoing temperament of the people, and the unsettled condition of the country so much of the time, induced a disinclination for sustained effort that became a characteristic of the race which has persisted to this day.

Among the major geographical factors, that of outlets to the sea also had its effect on the outlook of the people. Of the five important rivers whose valleys extend considerable distances inland, four (the Douro, Tajo, Guadiana, and Guadalquivir) empty into the Atlantic, and only one, the Ebro, into the Mediterranean. Of the first four, three have their estuaries along the Portuguese coast, forming harbors for important ports. Since the earliest days, therefore, Portugal's main outlets have been toward the Atlantic and the wide West. Spain has had to turn its face toward the Mediterranean, although in more recent times ports have been developed along the northern coast.

A Race for World Trade

Before the division of the peninsula into two distinct countries this was of small importance. Later, it had some psychological effect in influencing the outlook of the respective countries toward foreign trade and exploration. Portugal, with its eyes ever toward the Atlantic, looked to the Azores and the African Atlantic coast. Spain, when not preoccupied with internal strife, concerned itself with the development of Mediterranean sources of trade (either peacefully or by conquest), as it had from time out of mind. Not until Portugal had been in a more or less settled condition internally for two hundred years did Spain achieve the necessary unity to enable it to turn its attention to the establishment of an empire of its own.

This lag on the part of their Spanish cousins gave the Portuguese a head start in the race for world trade that was climaxed by the accidental discovery of the New World for Spain by Columbus in 1492. The Portuguese did discover something just as valuable to them at the time—a sea route to India—and only the merest chance kept them from bumping into South America long before they did. But here we are getting ahead of our story which concerns the development of the fifteenth century Spanish and Portuguese from barbarian tribes to the advanced civilizations which first spread from the Old World to the new one.

Phoenicians, Greeks, Carthaginians

Around 1100 B.C., then, other Mediterranean peoples began establishing tentative footholds in the homeland of the Iberian tribes. The first of these were the Phoenicians from the other end of the sea. The Phoenicians organized trading posts along the Mediterranean coast of Iberia, including a town they called Gades (now Cádiz) on the Atlantic side of the Gibraltar Straits.

These people were of Semitic stock, famed for their beautiful purple dyes, their fabrics, metalwork, and colored glass. They were great navigators, international traders, and colonizers. It was the Phoenicians who founded the ancient city of Carthage which occupied a site close to the modern Tunis in North Africa. Carthage was their chief colony, and a powerful influence in the Western Mediterranean even at this early date.

At this same time, Greek traders also began to establish small settlements on the Iberian coast, principally in the region now centered on Valencia, though they did wander as far as the mouth of the Douro River on the Atlantic coast. But even before the Greeks had obtained a firm foothold on the peninsula, the Carthaginians had begun to think more of conquest than of commerce. In their quarrels with Rome they cast covetous eyes on the mineral wealth of Iberia, which they needed to fight a war. The peninsula, with its gold, silver, copper, and lead mines, was a land occupied by semi-savage and disunited tribes who could, presumably, offer little organized resistance to invasion. They found, however, that the task was not so easy as it seemed, for it took them nine years to beat down the fierce opposition they encountered. Nevertheless, by 600 B.C., they had taken over a considerable portion of southern Iberia, and from 600 to 200 B.C. the lower fringe of the peninsula was subject to Carthage, which had outgrown its colonial status and formed an empire of its own.

This was but the beginning of a succession of invasions that was to turn the Iberian Peninsula into a melting pot of nations and the simple Iberians into highly complex individuals who were to become the fifteenth-century Spanish and Portuguese.

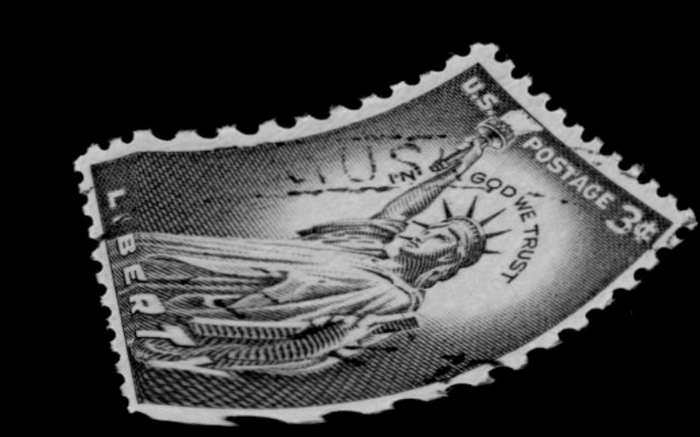

The Coming of the Celts

The next invasion came from the north when, around 500 B.C., the country was overrun by the Celts, a tall, blond people of Indo-European stock who came down through what is now France. Unable to conquer the Iberians living in the rugged mountain territory of the Pyrenees, the Celts drove south and west.

Over the centuries the Iberians absorbed these Celts, who intermarried with them to form a Celt-Iberian people. The northern Iberians, who had resisted the encroachment of the Celts, remained isolated in their mountain fastnesses, and from them are descended the Basques of today. They have changed little in overall characteristics from their forebears of 900 years ago.

The remaining Celt-Iberians were separated into four distinct groups—the Asturians, the Galicians, the Cantabrians, and the Lusitanians. The Lusitanians settled along the west coast, where they were eventually to form the Portuguese nation.

For almost four centuries the leaven of the Phoenician-Carthaginians worked to modify the characteristics of the southern Iberians. Large numbers of them intermarried, as did the Celts and Iberians throughout the rest of the country a century later.

The original primitive Iberians were a people of small stature, with dark hair and eyes, and skins of a delicate olive-white. It is thought that at some remote time they may have come from North Africa, and may therefore be distant kin of the Berbers who, so often in later centuries, tried to take their country away from them.

The descendants of the Phoenician-Iberians inherited both a fighting capacity and a trading instinct, a larger physique and a less insular outlook on life than the Celt-Iberians. They were easier to educate. In contrast, the Celt-Iberians retained their fierce independence, along with their sturdy fighting qualities, but became more peacefully inclined and less jealous of their neighbors. Celtic idealism softened their attitudes but not their vigor!

The Berbers varied in type, from the blue-eyed blonds

of the Atlas mountains to the black-skinned tribes of the oases. They were related both to the ancient Egyptians and the Ethiopians. Most of them were tall, olive-skinned, with curly hair, oval faces, and aquiline noses. They were distinctly an agricultural race, and by 1100 B.C. were well advanced toward civilization.

The Celt-Iberian tribes, on the other hand, were highly individualistic. Each group tended to keep to itself, and this lack of unity made it easier for the various invaders to overcome them one at a time. It also had the contrary effect of dragging out the wars of conquest, because the subjugation of one tribe had absolutely no effect on the rest. Each tribe had to be crushed separately; none of them knew when it was beaten. When the fight became hopeless, the men, and often the women, fought to the last, then dashed out their children's brains so that none remained to be enslaved.

Roman Expansion

The Romans discovered this when they decided to take over the peninsula at the beginning of the second century, B.C., and the wars against Carthage began with Iberia as the principal battleground. That is why it took hundreds of years for the Romans thoroughly to civilize the country. But "civilize" it they did even though they had to decimate the population first. This civilizing process was hastened somewhat by the widespread practice of Roman soldiers taking to themselves golden-skinned wives of Iberian blood.

With the coming of the Romans, the Celt-Iberians merely changed masters, but it was distinctly a change for the better. The Greeks had begun the education of these people by providing the rudiments of a written language in their alphabet. Rome, in the 700 years of its occupation, gave them law, the Latin language, civilized culture and social forms, a sound economy, Etruscan architecture, and the Christian religion. That was the period of their greatest advance, and marked the nearest approach to unification among the tribes.

For four centuries the peninsula was an important part of the Roman empire, and from it came some of the empire's greatest rulers, generals, teachers, writers, and poets. The emperors Trajan, Hadrian, Marcus Aurelius, and Theodosius, were all of Iberian origin. Hadrian made an incalculably important contribution to Iberian culture when he transplanted 50,000 Jewish families into the country. Since a large proportion of the population already had a remotely Semitic ancestry, the newcomers were readily assimilable and generally acceptable. Antagonisms based on religion or origin were a much later development, and many of the Jewish people married into Christian or even pagan, households. But the Empire itself was not fated to last.

Rome's control of the Iberian Peninsula came to an end rather more quickly than it had begun. At the beginning of the fifth century, A.D., a horde of Germanic tribes descended upon the Peninsula from the north, and for the next three hundred years Iberia was ruled by cultures far inferior to that of Rome.

First came the Vandals, the Alans, and the Suevis. Crossing the Rhine, they devastated France and poured into the Iberian Peninsula. Four hundred years of comparative peace had weakened the people's resistance. Many of their finest warriors had joined the Roman legions, and gone off to fight Rome's battles in Britain and other distant parts. So the Suevis and some of the Vandals settled in the North; the Alans and the rest of the Vandals drove on down the West coast to the South.

Rule of the Visigoths

But theirs was a short-lived triumph. In less than five years another and more powerful invader—the Visigoths—came along to dispute possession with them. The Visigoths, originally hailing from Scandinavia, had been allies of the Romans, and some of them were Christians. Having conveniently fallen out with their allies, they not only sacked Rome but went on to capture the east coast of southern Gaul (France). Pushing on down the east coast of the peninsula, they took Barcelona. Driving south, they forced the Vandals to leave for Africa in haste. The Suevis they squeezed into a pocket in the northwest corner of the peninsula and thereafter apparently ignored them.

By A.D. 623, practically all of the peninsula was under the rule of the Visigoths. Soon, all that was left of the Roman civilization was a modified Christianity, some political institutions, and the remnants of Roman law that would persist for centuries to come.

The Visigoths ruled Iberia for 300 years, and for a long time the Church was the only worthwhile unifying factor. The Visigoths, however, were Aryan Christians, and those of the Roman church looked upon them as heretics, as they did the increasing number of Jews whom the Visigoths welcomed as useful citizens. Fortunately for themselves, and for national unity, the Gothic ruler and his son, together with other leaders, became members of the Roman Church. This act helped to stabilize the country in a time of unrest, but the beginnings of intolerance were becoming all too evident as the Church gained in power.

The rank and file of the Visigoths placed small stock in organized religion, and the color of a man's skin meant little to them. They were the most tolerant of mortals when left to their own devices. But with the growing power of the Roman Church in both spiritual and temporal affairs of the nation, religious belief became important. The Church could only exercise full control over its own followers; it was therefore necessary to discourage all other religions. From that day the Church continued to be one of the most significant factors in Iberian life.

In the 300 years of Visigothic rule there was much intermarriage between the various peoples that made up the population. Although the Gothic tribes did not represent an advance in culture, they were both vigorous and progressive. They were good organizers, even though minor civil wars were common. They established admirable laws and strengthened the moral character of the people as a whole through encouragement of religious beliefs. But, in spite of all this, there was a great deal of disaffection among the nobles and those in authority. This discontent spread to the various classes of the populace who had no strong unifying bond such as a national consciousness, and no inspiring common purpose.

Invasion from Africa

This was the weak spot in the body politic, and when the next invasion was launched from Africa, resistance on a national scale was ineffective and defections among leaders were many. Actually, a few of the Gothic nobles, together with the Bishop of Seville and some of the oppressed Iberian Jews, all had a hand in making things easy for the invaders. These felt that any change at all could only be for the better.

The first Moslem invasion began in A.D. 710, and the dark-skinned Semitic Moslems, known as Moors, occupied the Iberian Peninsula for the next eight hundred years. In less than a decade the conquest was virtually complete. In contrast to the growing rise of intolerance under the Christian Goths, the Moorish rule was marked by great freedom in the practice of religion. The lot of the minorities, especially the Jews, was greatly improved. The conquerors, however, suffered both from internal disunity and attacks by the small number of unconquered Christian Iberians they had driven into the mountains of the north.

The Moorish forces were made up of several rival groups who quarreled constantly and, on occasion, fought bitterly. Had it not been for the fact that the Christians also were divided, the re-conquest, as it is called, would have taken a lot less time than it did. Not until the tenth century were the disorders brought under control and some semblance of unity achieved.

In the comparative peace that ensued, both agriculture and industry flourished, and the arts were encouraged. Beautiful houses and palaces were built, and the city of Córdoba became the cultural center of Western Europe, with its great library of 400,000 volumes, its 900 bath houses, its 600 mosques, and its great university which drew students from all parts of the continent.

Medicine and mathematics were subjects of intense

study, but the clergy frowned on the pursuit of knowledge in the fields of astronomy and philosophy, for reasons that are not hard to divine. The Moors delighted in art in all its forms, especially in decoration, architecture, and music, and the industrial arts flourished. And all of this at a time when Paris and London were dirty and squalid towns!

But the northern Christian states were growing more powerful year by year, and in the thirteenth century they united to drive out the Moors. Little by little they reconquered territory. The expanding Christian states were each ruled by a king, and some of these states became united under one ruler, thus gaining in strength.

Among the territories first recaptured was that now occupied by Portugal. The loyalty of the Portuguese nobles to the king, and the reduction of the powers of the Church, brought unity and peace to this region, after the aggressions of the neighboring province of Castile were stopped. The Spanish states were not so fortunate, and disorders resulting in lack of political unity kept Spain in a state of turmoil for another two hundred years.

Expansion and Bigotry

It was not till the middle of the fifteenth century that the final step toward internal tranquillity was taken by the union of the two great states, Aragon and Castile. This union was effected through the marriage of the rulers, Queen Isabella of Castile and King Ferdinand of Aragon. Under the joint rule of these two sovereigns, Spain was at last ready for the consolidation of the entire country, and the beginning of an era of progress, expansion—and unparalleled bigotry. There remained only the final expulsion of the Moors who still clung to the city of Granada and its surrounding territory. This was accomplished in 1492—a memorable year in history.

Unfortunately for Ferdinand and Isabella, they did not have the wholehearted support of the Spanish grandees in their efforts to establish peace and prosperity. The nobles were fighting men and peace would take away their opportunities for gold and glory. Law and order meant the loss of too many privileges, though neither they nor the clergy were called upon to pay taxes. That was the prerogative of the newly developing middle class and the free laborers.

The banishment of the Moors was not an unmixed blessing. They were the nation's chief food producers—the agriculturists and cattle breeders—and this loss served to emphasize the impoverished condition of the country generally. In a further step toward achieving national unity, the rulers sought to impose a universal religion on all their subjects. This resulted in the expulsion, absorption, or murder of a great number of Jews, procedures applauded by a large section of the population who were jealous of their relative prosperity, and their hold on industry, commerce, and finance.

This step, while it may have contributed to the influence of the Church and therefore the State over the people, nevertheless added to the poverty of the country, and benefited no one. On the contrary, it fanned the flames of intolerance, which eventually found its finest flowering among the Christians themselves in the form of the Holy Inquisition.

This, then, was the background and origin of the Spanish Conquistadors who ravaged the "Indies," and their

Portuguese blood brothers who brought the sword and the Cross to the unsuspecting savages in Brazil.

In origin, as we have shown, the Portuguese and Spaniards differed but little. They were alike the product of the fusion of contrasting cultures and mixed races—the Mediterraneans, Nordics, Semites; the pagans, Moslems, Jews, and Christians; the warriors, artists, traders, lawmakers, and organizers. But most of their history had been marked by unrest, by wars and disputes, invasions and massacres, by radical changes in government systems and dominant religions.

For long there was no middle class, only peons and the nobility. And in the end no man cared to permit himself to be classed with the serfs or even tradesmen. Every man's ambition was to be a noble, or a reasonable facsimile thereof. This was the cult of the hidalgo. Work was tabu if other means of existence could be found, and often if they could not.

A clue to this trait of the Spanish (and Portuguese) character is contained in the one little word "dignidad." It is translated in English as "dignity," but it means a great deal more. It is the expression of an attitude toward life and all mankind. It is the sentiment which debases even honest work, and makes it impossible for the gentleman to forget he is *caballero*—and a man on horseback does not do anything remotely resembling manual labor even for pleasure. *Dignidad* is preserved by confining one's pursuits to those things that are considered the privileges of the wealthy and the well-born. And all social and business affairs must be conducted on that plane.

By the fifteenth century both the country and the nobles were impoverished. But trade and industry—the perquisites of the Moors and the Jews—were despised, though many of the leading families of the country had Jewish or Moorish blood or both. Men of independence had long lived by the sword and the labors of the less fortunate. In a united country there was no longer a demand for their services; there was nothing that the proud citizen could do but join the Army or the Church. But even in the Army there was little occasion for the exercise of the arts of war. The Moors and the Jews were gone, and the Crusades long over. The nobles were ripe for opportunities to smite the infidels in the New World, especially if there was loot to be had along with the glory.

Such was the background, the origin, and the character of the men who set out to rob an empire of its treasure and subdue a great continent for their King and the Holy Mother Church. This was the casqued and breastplated Spanish conquistador, lithe and supple as his Damascened Toledo blade with its delicate tracery of inlaid gold; a slender sword that could be flexed, tip to pommel, like a polished steel spring. Yet all of the conquistadors were not alike to the eye.

Their differences of origin were evident from their appearance. Some were tall, dark and cadaverous, like Pizarro and many of his companions. Others were ruddy, light-skinned and blue-eyed, with hair of flaming red like that of Vasco Nuñez de Balboa. Others were of all shades and degrees of darkness or fairness between the two extremes. But, whatever their physical characteristics, they were united in a common aim that was to decide the future of a continent and the shape of its civilization to come.

THE WHITE MAN TAKES OVER

CHAPTER 4

THE WHITE MAN TAKES OVER

IF THERE EVER WAS SUCH A THING AS an accidental empire, the development of South America by the Spaniards and Portuguese furnishes a matchless example. The Spaniards who first came to South America did not represent the Crown, and they had no intention of founding an empire. They organized and financed their own expeditions and sought only gold, glory, and adventure. Treasure was the magnet that drew them on, and Chance played a major role in deciding which parts of South America they were to settle first.

Later on, luck and a little shrewd bargaining divided the continent almost equally between the Spanish and Portuguese, and thereby determined the fate of millions of brown men, all unaware of the calamity that was to descend upon them. The reasons for which South America was subjugated, the methods by which this was effected, and the spirit in which it was done, are interesting because of what they reveal about the men who performed that herculean task. And all of this must be considered against the background of conditions in Europe at that time and in the world the Europeans knew.

Unlike other historic conquests, this one was not a national undertaking in which the forces of one state were pitted against those of another. No great armies were involved on the side of the invaders; only a few pitifully equipped fighting men who made up in determination and courage what they lacked in numbers and arms.

The important facts about the later colonization were the manner in which it was carried out, the regions first settled, and the spread of influence and physical possession from that time on.

In the beginning, there was a great deal of confusion as to who owned what. Columbus discovered South America for the Spanish, but thought that it was part of Asia because a Florentine astronomer named Toscanelli had calculated the earth's circumference as being one-seventh smaller than it is. Ptolemy, the Greco-Egyptian geographer, had made a similar miscalculation thirteen hundred years before, so Columbus can hardly be blamed for his mistaken assumption. Had he really found a short route to the Indies, that in itself would have been fit cause for rejoicing among the peoples of Europe.

Mediterranean Blockade

Since the dawn of history, the group of Mediterranean countries, which constituted most of the known world at that time, had traded with India via the long overland route through Turkey and Iran. In 1453 the Turks had captured Constantinople, and had begun to shut off the age-old trade routes to the East. Besides bringing commerce with the Indies to a standstill, this blockade cut off the Mediterranean countries from their principal source of spices. Now these spices were no mere luxuries. They were among the most important items of commerce in those days, when refrigeration was unknown. Spices were needed for the preservation of many kinds of foods, and for making palatable those that could not be kept fresh. Civilized living was practically impossible without them, because everybody ate large quantities of meat and had few vegetables to go with them. Some spices took the place of vegetables.

Spices, of course, were not all the Indies provided. There were to be had rich cargoes of gems, perfumes, porcelains, rugs, and gums, and for a long time their distribution throughout the Mediterranean had been monopolized by the merchants of Venice and Genoa. This was one reason that the Portuguese had done a tremendous amount of exploration long before Columbus was born.

Henry the Navigator

While the Spaniards were still busy trying to reconcile the warring factions in their own country, Portugal was seeking prosperity through international trade, always with a weather eye open for a little conquest on the side if anything should turn up worth seizing. In this the Portuguese mariners were encouraged by a scion of their royal house, one of the truly great men of his time, Prince Henry the Navigator.

A son of King João of Portugal (John the Great), Prince Henry gave little thought to the throne. His mother was an Englishwoman, Philippa of Lancaster, and from her he inherited an overwhelming passion for the sea. He believed his country's future lay in the conquest of the ocean as a highway to far-off lands.

In 1419 Prince Henry made his home on the most southwesterly point of the Iberian Peninsula, and built there an observatory and a school of navigation. Under his direction, voyages of exploration were made out into the Atlantic and along the African coast for the next forty-one years. The islands of the Azores and Madeira, first found in the fourteenth century, were rediscovered and settled. Cape Verde was reached and named, and the coast of Africa as far south as six degrees above the Equator.

Prince Henry died in 1460, probably disappointed that his navigators had not made the discovery nearest his heart—the fabled African kingdom of the Christian ruler, Prester John, with whom he hoped to form an alliance to fight the Turks and free the Holy Land. Neither had they found the "golden land" of Timbuktu.

After Prince Henry's death, the Portuguese spent thirty-seven years finding their way around the southern tip of Africa. It was the great seaman-explorer, Vasco da Gama, who first sailed beyond the Cape of Good Hope and on to India, thus giving the Portuguese a private trade route to the Moluccas, the Spice Islands of the East. When da Gama returned to Portugal with his shipload of oriental treasures, another expedition was at once prepared to follow the same route, this time under the control of Pedro Alvares Cabral.

The Pope Draws a Line

Meanwhile, in order to legalize their claim to the "Indies," the Spanish sovereigns, Ferdinand and Isabella,

good deal about the South American coast, but found no gold, gems, or even spices. All it did take home was a cargo of brazilwood from which useful red and purple dyes could be made. It was from this wood that Brazil got its name.

Having all of India and the East with which to trade, it is not surprising that the Portuguese thought little of Brazil and its naked savages. In the years that followed, they sent a few ships to bring home more dyewood and to dump ashore an occasional *degredado*—a convict or other undesirable citizen. This last was a simple and easy way of finding out whether or not the natives were hospitable or cannibalistic, and if there was likelihood of treasure being found in the interior.

But while the Portuguese were indifferent, or too preoccupied elsewhere to do much about Brazil, other nations, who did not recognize the Pope's authority to parcel out the earth between Spain and Portugal, were more curious. Between 1503 and 1508 several French expeditions were made to the Brazilian coast and up the rivers. The Spanish likewise were interested in learning more about the lower end of the continent's east coast, and hoped to find a passage through to the west.

These activities convinced the King of Portugal that something would have to be done to preserve his rights to the continental coast from the Orinoco to the Rio de la Plata. Accordingly, he dispatched a fleet of six ships to patrol Brazilian waters and chase away intruders. In their first encounter with the trespassers this force took 300 Frenchmen as prisoners to the fort they had established near present-day Pernambuco. Shortly thereafter, the fleet went home and the fort was abandoned with the Frenchmen in possession. Meanwhile, various individuals and groups who had been left ashore from time to time made friends with the Indians and married Indian women. Some of them had quite large families and formed small settlements of their own long before the first organized groups of colonists arrived.

Balboa and Pizarro

While Portugal was thus playing dog-in-the-manger with Brazil, Spanish adventurers were organizing minor treasure hunts on the Caribbean coast. Among these adventurers was Francisco Pizarro, an illiterate soldier of fortune, a former Estremaduran swineherd, and now a survivor of a colony of 300 that had been reduced by Indian arrows, starvation, and shipwreck to 30 not particularly worthy souls. These formed the nucleus of a new colony, founded by Vasco Nuñez de Balboa and Fernandez de Enciso, which was called Santa María la Antigua del Darién.

Within a very short time, the ruthless Balboa had got rid of Enciso, forcibly married the daughter of an Indian chief to secure his alliance, and had taken over control of the territory himself. He then set out to explore the surrounding country in the hope of discovering gold, of which there were many rumors but little evidence.

In 1511 Balboa, with Pizarro at his heels, called upon an Indian cacique whose chance remarks were to lead to the conquest of Peru. In accordance with a pleasant custom, the Indian offered his guests a quantity of gold objects as parting gifts. Disgusted at the mad scramble which ensued among the visitors, the chief's son threw the gold to the ground. "If this is what you crave," he cried, "I can tell you where you will find all your hearts desire. Where gold is so plentiful that the people use golden vessels from which to eat and drink."

Balboa and Pizarro eagerly drank in the details. Beyond the mountains of the isthmus, they were told, lay a great sea. Somewhere south of it was the rich land. This was interesting news, but it might or might not be the truth. They had heard such tales before, and there were many obstacles in the way of reaching it. Expeditions were dangerous, difficult to organize, and expensive. Besides, they must have ships, horses, and many soldiers to attempt to conquer the great country the Indian had described.

Balboa Finds the South Sea

It was two years before these men were able to learn whether or not the story of the sea beyond the mountains was true. But finally, in September, 1513, Balboa, accompanied by Pizarro, led a desperate march across the isthmus of Panama and sighted the mysterious South Sea, which he took possession of in the name of the Spanish crown.

News of this discovery reached Spain at about the same time that word arrived of the fabulous treasures that another conquistador, Hernando Cortes, had found in Mexico, and the gold rush was on. The king appointed a governor for Darien to organize expeditions to the south. This man, Pedro Arias d'Avila, known better as Pedrarias the Cruel, was besieged by thousands of footloose adventurers anxious to garner a rich harvest of gold and gems. When he set sail for Panama, 1,500 of these brocaded cavaliers in search of gay adventure went with him. But instead of riches, they found hunger, disease, and death. In one month, 700 of them were dead from fever and starvation.

In the meantime, Pedrarias had moved across the isthmus and founded the town of Panama, after chopping off Balboa's head and massacring all the Indians he could lay hands on. After Balboa's death, Pizarro retired to a cattle ranch which he had acquired with the help of another adventurer, Diego de Almagro.

Several minor expeditions had set out to find the rich country to the south, but none had succeeded. Nevertheless, the evidence of incredible riches mounted with each quest, and finally Pizarro could no longer resist temptation to try his hand. He and Almagro sold their farm and went into partnership with the Vicar of Panama, Father Hernando de Luque, who provided most of the money for the expedition.

There is no need to go into the trials and misfortunes that befell Pizarro and Almagro, or their repeated failures and near disaster. Many of their men were killed, and Almagro lost an eye, but this did not deter the tough and ruthless Pizarro. The men learned what they wanted to know, and returned to Panama with enough gold, emeralds, Indians, and llamas to convince that priest that, with sufficient men, they could undertake the conquest that would bring them untold riches. But de Luque had no more money, and the governor was scornful of the results they had attained at so great a cost of lives. And so Pizarro took his gold ornaments and llamas and went back to Spain to ask the help of King Charles.

Since he had little to lose and stood to gain considerable revenues from this promising new source of wealth, the King agreed to back the expedition. Pizarro and his associates were invested with various titles and powers, as well as stupendous salaries which they were to derive from the treasure they found. The priest was made a bishop, and was given charge of the souls of the Indians that Pizarro and Almagro might subdue without slaying.

The Conquest of Peru

From among his kinsmen, boyhood friends, and a further collection of unsavory characters, Pizarro raised a substantial company of poor but proud cutthroats, eager to follow him to the fabulous land of Peru. Pizarro had grabbed off all the highest titles for himself, bringing along four villainous half-brothers to share the spoils.

This did not please Almagro and the two leaders quarreled bitterly. Because of the dissension between their chiefs, few really capable men could be induced to join the enterprise. But this time the fates were in Pizarro's favor, and in 1532 he established the first Spanish settlement in Peru. Eighteen weeks later, he launched the conquest of Peru in earnest with the treacherous murder of the ruler of the Incas, Atahualpa.

We need not concern ourselves with the gory details of the slaughter of the Incas and the vicious attack upon a friendly people that was to result in the wrecking of the empire. These things have been described in countless history books and related with gusto in many a tale of adventure. What we *are* concerned with is tracing the distribution of the Spanish forces throughout the continent, and the settlements they founded as a prelude to wholesale exploitation of South American inhabitants and resources.

In the beginning, the Spaniards were quite prepared to cart off their loot to Spain, where they could enjoy the proceeds of their conquest in comfort and luxury. But the riches of the ready-made native empires they encountered, and the difficulties that they had in subduing the owners of that wealth, together with the vast extent of the plunder, made it necessary for them to create more or less permanent establishments for the collection of wealth and its shipment to the homeland.

When all the visible treasure had been confiscated and divided, however, the government became interested in squeezing still more wealth out of the country. Therefore, the next step of the conquerors was to seize the sources of supply—the gold and emerald mines—and to force the Indians to work them. This involved close and continuous supervision, as well as the maintaining of authority by force. This was the primary reason why these Spaniards founded towns and set up local governments. It was a long time before the conquistadors and the later settlers brought their women from Spain and set up permanent homes. As a consequence, the beginnings of civilized society that they established did not at first extend beyond the towns that they settled and maintained.

The first town that Pizarro established in Peru was San Miguel de Piura, near the point where he first landed. A number of Indians were allotted to each don as slaves, and they were at once set to work to build houses. Plots of land were distributed among the Spaniards, and municipal government was established. A few months later, after various bloody battles, Cuzco was taken, and a rash of ornate Spanish style churches began to appear among the ruins of the ancient temples.

In 1535, Pizarro founded Lima, the City of Kings, on the coast almost midway between Lake Titicaca and the Guayas River. This was the Spanish capital, and the strategic port through which the wealth of Peru was to be funneled to the King's coffers in Spain, and into the pockets of his loyal subjects who had brought the sword and the Cross to the "hopeless heretycks" of the New World.

Valdivia Drinks the Molten Gold

In the same year, as a consequence of an undeclared war between Pizarro and himself, Diego de Almagro began the conquest of lower Peru, which today is called Chile. His utter failure did not deter Pizarro's Field Marshal, Pedro de Valdivia, from attempting the same thing five years later. With better luck, and some narrow escapes from annihilation, Valdivia founded the city of Santiago, as well as another town which he called La Serena, near the present site of Coquimbo. A little later, as time went with the conquistadors, he laid out several small settlements and the town of Concepción, which was later called Penco. But for every foot of Chilean soil that he took, Valdivia paid dearly in Spanish lives.

In the end, a young Indian boy named Lautaro, whom Valdivia and his Spanish mistress had reared, turned up as the indomitable leader of the Araucanians. Wise to Spanish ways, Lautaro led his men to victory. The natives wiped out the Spanish forces, killing every man except Valdivia and a friar named Padre Pozo. There are many stories of Valdivia's end, one of the least bloodthirsty being that his death occurred from a draught of molten gold—the metal for which he had ruthlessly sacrificed a great many other lives than his own.

Civil war in Peru halted any further expansion for several years. Meanwhile, a number of towns had begun to grow along the Caribbean coast, such as Santa Marta (1525), and Cartagena (1533), which were the main northern outlets for treasure to Spain, and the gates through which ever more and more gold-hungry adventurers poured.

In 1536, the governor of this region, Pedro de Lugo, decided to explore the Magdalena River. An expedition was arranged with Gonzalo Jiménez de Quesada, the chief magistrate, at its head. After months of incredible hardships, Quesada reached the Sabána de Bogotá and set about subduing the friendly Chibcha Indians. As we mentioned earlier, he found sufficient gold and emeralds, and a great deal of food, which made it not only interesting but profitable to stay there, even if he was unable to track down the mysterious El Dorado of which men still dreamed.

Shortly thereafter, two other expeditions arrived on the scene, one led by Sebastian de Belalcázar, fresh from the conquest of Quito, the other, by Nicholaus Federmann, a German, from Venezuela, both of whom were hot on the trail of El Dorado. The first arrival, Jiménez de Quesada, paid Federmann a sum of money to withdraw from the hunt. Belalcázar, the proud Spaniard, was satisfied with retaining the territory of Popayán where he established the towns of Neiva and Timana.

Orellana Sails the Amazon

In 1539, Gonzalo Pizarro, one of the infamous Francisco's many half-brothers, set out from Quito to find the fabled Land of Cinnamon. By the time he and his men had reached the jungles of Ecuador's Oriente, their situation was desperate. On the banks of the Napo River these sick and hungry soldiers performed the minor miracle of building a boat which would carry fifty men. Pizarro's second in command, Francisco de Orellana, was put in charge of this boat, which was loaded to capacity, and was sent down the river in search of food. Instead of finding provisions for the wanderers, Orellana was swept down the Napo and on to the broad bosom of a mighty river that later came to be called the Amazon. Eventually, he and his party arrived at the mouth of the Amazon, then sailed along the north coast of South America, finally landing at what is now Port of Spain on the island of Trinidad.

To us, at the moment, the importance of Orellana's discovery lies in the fact that Spain claimed the territory, he had traversed. This fact alarmed the Portuguese to such an extent that they sent a captain-general, Thomé de Souza, to protect this area. He landed in Bahia in 1549, with a few soldiers and Jesuit priests, and 400 convicts on whom fell the distinction of becoming the founders and populators of this historic city.

Brazil's Beginnings

Thomé de Souza was the first representative of the Crown to be sent to Brazil, and his arrival marked the beginning of organized colonization by Portugal. Long before that, however, Brazil had been divided into thirteen captaincies, in the hope that each of the feudal landlords who ruled over them would not only take steps to protect his own concession, but extend it as far west as possible, preferably into Inca territory where they could tap the Spanish sources of gold. Any activities these men may have initiated in this direction, however, were cut short by the Spanish incursion into the River Plata area. They therefore contented themselves with seeking means of putting the coastal lands to some productive use.

Since there were few settlers along the coast, and as the few Indians who could readily be captured did not make good slaves (the Portuguese never did learn that it is the Indian *women* who do the manual labor), the new landlords were forced to turn to Africa for the free labor they required.

In their searches for uses to which this new land could be put, the Portuguese experimented with sugar cane which they brought from Madeira. To operate sugar plantations, which were destined to become the country's first great source of wealth, they imported Negro slaves from the Guinea Coast. This was in 1532, long before any systematic attempt had been made to enslave the Indians—a project that called for organized military campaigns and was never wholly successful.

Since the slaves could not be expected to work without supervision, overseers were recruited from Portugal's peasant class. Colonization was given an unexpected impetus in 1536 by the introduction of the Holy Inquisition into Portugal. The persecution of heretics and Jews (among which were included some of the richest Portuguese families and leading business men), drove large numbers to seek refuge in Brazil.

Therefore, the first colonists were composed of all classes and stations—the noblemen or *fidalgos*, the Jews, the peasants, and the Negroes. Among these the proportion of women was very small, and many of the colonists took to themselves Indian women, either as wives or concubines, the result in either case being offspring of mixed blood. This situation was somewhat relieved in 1551 by the arrival of a large number of female orphans of noble parentage. Sent by the Queen, with a dowry of one horse and one Negro apiece, these girls were distributed among the officers and officials. This practice was continued for several years, and numbers of orphan boys were also shipped to the colony to be educated by the Jesuits.

Cabot and Mendoza

In spite of all this activity, the actual number of Portuguese in Brazil for a long time was small, and they were probably outnumbered by their slaves ten to one! For almost two centuries the colonists were confined to the coast, and little exploration of the interior was carried out. Meanwhile, however, there had been a lot of activity in the River Plata region. Exploration of this area began in 1515, and extended to parts of present-day Bolivia and Paraguay. But little interest was displayed by the world at large till Sebastian Cabot came out of the wilderness in 1530 with a four-years' accumulation of silver and gold. This was sufficient to indicate to the Spanish people that the shores of the Rio de la Plata were really worth colonizing, in spite of the hostile Indians.

The first on the scene was Pedro Mendoza, who arrived in 1534 with eleven ships loaded down with 2500 colonists, cattle, seed, and agricultural implements, plus a fierce determination to find a way to the Inca empire from the east. A fort was built at Santa María de Buenos Aires, but Indian attacks rendered the neighborhood unhealthy, and the colony was moved up the Paraná River to a place they called Corpus Christi, which today is Asunción, capital of Paraguay.

Mendoza's expedition had been planned by the Spanish Crown long before the news arrived in Spain of Pizarro's success. Spain had heard of the Portuguese move to expand westward, a move that might well have put an end to Pizarro's drive through Peru. The prime purpose of the expedition, therefore, was to take over the mountain of silver that Cabot had reported, and which had been raided by Alejo García, a survivor of the ill-fated expedition of Juan Diaz de Solis who discovered the Mar Dulce (freshwater sea), as he called the Plata River, in 1615. De Solis was killed, and one of his ships was wrecked on Santa Catharina Island off the coast of Brazil.

Among the eleven survivors of this wreck was this Alejo García, who immediately began to occupy his time learning the Guaraní language from the Indians. The Guaranís told him of the great kingdom in the mountains ruled by the Rey Blanco (white king). In 1524 García, accompanied by four other crew members, walked across Brazil to Paraguay, and apparently thought little of the feat. At a Guaraní settlement he persuaded every able-bodied man to go with him to invade the territory of the Rey Blanco, with the idea of securing what booty they could. Thus, for the first time, the Guaranís learned that silver was something that was worth fighting, suffering, and dying for.

The five whites and 2,000 Indians then paddled 400

miles up the Paraguay River and set off across the Chaco Boreal towards the Andes—a territory devoid of navigable rivers, and full of hostile Indians when it was not flooded and impassable. Thanks to the Guaranís, they reached Charcas in the territory of the Caracaras Indians where the Potosí mines were. Recovering from the initial shock of the raid on their territory, the Caracaras chased the Guaranís and their white leaders down the mountains again, but not before they had been relieved of a large amount of silver and gold.

García later attempted to organize another sortie into the Inca domain, but he was killed, some say eaten, by the Guaranís before he could get away. It was at this time that Sebastian Cabot, on his roundabout way to the Spice Islands, stopped at Pernambuco where he heard of García's find. Instead of going on to India, Cabot decided to explore the River Plata to see if he could find a water route to Potosí. He did not succeed in penetrating the continent very far, but he did pick up enough precious metal from the Indians to arouse the interest of the authorities in Spain, and to encourage Mendoza to believe that he could accomplish a great deal more than establish the few settlements for which he had contracted.

Between 1536 and 1573, other towns were established, including Santa Fé and Córdoba, and in 1580 a town was built on the site of the original fort at Buenos Aires. With a degree of peace achieved between the colonists and the Indians, many settlers took to themselves wives from among the Guaraní tribes. As a consequence, the Guaraní language became the common tongue of the Paraguayans.

This, then, was the manner in which the white man came to South America—his aim plunder and his methods indescribably cruel and vicious. In the beginning, the conquest was in the hands of avaricious adventurers who endeavored to force Christianity and their own brand of civilization on the inferior races by means of torture, mutilation, rape, and treacherous murder. Pillage was followed by slavery, and the progressive native civilizations were destroyed, with nothing to replace them but serfdom and degradation. Moreover, the Europeans brought with them diseases hitherto unknown on the continent. Smallpox raged among the Indians and killed far more than the whips of the mine overseers. But in a measure, the Indian had his revenge, for many a proud don was to succumb to the worst scourge of all, a disease that spread like wildfire through the ranks of common soldiers and captains alike—syphilis!

The ill-treatment of the Indian was from the beginning a matter of grave concern to the rulers of Spain and Portugal. They never countenanced slavery of the Indians, except in the case of cannibals or prisoners of war. It needs no imagination to picture how quickly cannibalism spread among the brown men, or how many suddenly declared war on their protectors. The padres, too, objected to the enslavement of Indians, though they had no such compunctions regarding Negroes, who had been fair game for the Iberian "blackbirders" for many a year. The efforts of the Crown and Church to stamp out this evil met with little success, particularly in Brazil, for a very long time.

Two important results of the demand for Indian slaves were the killing of large numbers of men, and the breeding of a whole new race of mestizos by the women. At one time, thousands of these mestizos roamed the highlands of Brazil, and none were more ready to kill and sell into slavery the kinfolk of their mothers.

The Contribution of the Indian

In searching for clues to the nature of the various peoples who were the victims in these sadistic orgies of the sixteenth and seventeenth centuries, there are a number of things to be borne in mind. One is that in the civilization which the Spaniards destroyed, very few of the individual Indians had reached the cultural level that their social organization represented. For instance, the ordinary people of the Inca empire were barbarians, subject to strict rule and purposely kept in an uneducated state so that they would not become overly ambitious. On the other hand, there arose from their ranks many who achieved high positions of authority under the ruling class, and others who developed great skills as artists and artisans.

All of the great achievements of the builders, architects, and workers in gold and textiles were undoubtedly of the lower class. Given the opportunity, they would have contributed far more to the culture than they did, and the whole Inca civilization would have risen to even greater heights. The Incas, themselves, as previously pointed out, stemmed from a few individuals who had risen above their fellows, and beneath their feathered cloaks and fillets they were still Indians like the rest.

Their empire was achieved by conquest and maintained by force under a highly organized political system. By the time the Spaniards arrived this had broken down to such an extent that a bloody civil war between two rival Incas was just being concluded. This much simplified the task of the conquistadors who found unexpected allies in some of the subject groups within the Inca domain.

The same principles apply to the Chibchas, who were

less spectacular in their organization and symbolism, but culturally on a level with the Incas. The Araucanians, of course, were border-line savages, but with the makings of a culture that would not have been founded on the subjection of the masses to a ruling class. They were individualists who recognized the value of cooperation for the common good, but refused to bow the neck to any yoke. Theirs was the nearest approach to democracy that any native South American culture ever achieved.

Throughout the rest of the continent, the Indians varied almost from tribe to tribe in their level of culture—from the most primitive savages to the organized, village-dwelling agriculturists.

Without the Europeans and the things they brought with them, this civilizing process would have been longer delayed. In spite of its immense size, the continent had little land suitable for agriculture, and the Indians had no animals such as cattle, sheep, and horses to whom the vast areas of pasture lands would have been of benefit. And most of them, with the exception of the Incas, knew nothing of fertilization. When the land became less productive they moved elsewhere, or suffered from limited supplies of food. Moving meant, as a rule, conflict with other groups, and minor wars were constantly in progress from one end of the continent to the other. We must, therefore, in fairness to the European invaders, not picture the aboriginal South America as a pagan paradise into which they brought only misery and death. Even under the better organized societies, the primitive peoples knew want, hunger, and oppression.

With the coming of the white men (and the black), conditions changed rapidly for many of these Indians.

Some of them were Christianized. They were often herded together, and thousands sickened and died. Others, however, progressed toward civilization at a pace that is cause for wonder.

Mendoza brought horses into Paraguay in 1534. Seven hundred of them were turned loose when Mendoza abandoned Buenos Aires and moved upriver to Asunción, and in a few years thousands of them romped and galloped over the plains. Indians, who had discovered that a Spaniard on horseback was not a centaur, captured horses for themselves. Overnight their hunting methods were revolutionized—the Indian was as fleet as the animals he pursued. From that time on the Indians learned to ride as soon as they could walk. They used horses for food, their skins for clothing, tents, and rawhide ropes. Thus began tribal prosperity and leisure for development in other ways; the natives became meat-eaters and herdsmen. Life was simpler and much more fun. In such simple ways may civilization begin.

Social Distinctions in America

Before turning our attention to peoples of the various modern countries that developed from these unpromising beginnings, it is necessary to consider two important factors that influenced their growth. One of these is that during these early days in both Portuguese and Spanish territories, foreigners were not permitted to enter. Equally important is the second fact that Spain also restricted immigration of its own people to the colony. After the first shock of the invasion was over and the country pacified, the Spanish authorities sought by every means to bar entry to the very kind of individual that had organized the conquest—the adventurers in search of easy wealth! Thereafter, every Spanish immigrant was required to satisfy the authorities as to his integrity, and his allegiance to the tenets of the Church.

For those seeking profits through commerce, the attractions of the colony were small, and manufacturing was almost non-existent. All manual labor was performed by Indians, mestizos, or Negroes, and most of these were employed on the vast estates, in farming or in the mines. As a result of this policy, immigration was limited to less than 1,500 individuals a year for the next hundred years or so. Consequently, there was never a prosperous middle class in South America such as forms the backbone of countries elsewhere.

This does not mean that there were no social distinctions among the Spaniards. Far from it. The white population was soon divided into two distinct and competing classes—those that were born in Spain and those born on the continent. In a very few years the American-born Spaniards (who were called *criollos,* i.e., creoles) far outnumbered the Spanish émigres. But those hailing from Spain were looked upon with greater favor by the home government and held a virtual monopoly of the higher offices, both in the State and Church.

The creoles, on the other hand, constituted the majority of large-scale farmers and cattlemen, the important merchants, and the professional classes. This discrimination led to friction between the Spaniards and the creoles whom the Spaniards treated as inferiors. This state of affairs was encouraged rather then deplored by the Crown for the simple reason that the two elements were not likely to combine to throw off the Spanish rule. So long as they opposed and fought each other, the colony was safe.

This attitude, and the trade restrictions imposed on the colony, actually did far more harm than good, as the Spanish Government discovered too late. By the time changes were made, the South Americans were preparing to throw off European control which, from the first, had not been designed to further their interests or encourage their aims.

A R G E N T I N A

ARGENTINA:

CHAPTER 5

LAND OF THE PAMPAS

THE FABULOUS SILVER MOUNTAINS which lured so many Spanish adventurers to their doom gave Argentina its name. But it was the rich soil of those vast grassy plains, the *pampas,* and not the precious metal that enabled it to grow into one of the largest food exporting countries in the world. This Land of Silver, stretching 2300 miles from Bolivia's silver mountains to the point where Tierra del Fuego bathes its feet in the Antarctic Ocean, is the second largest country of South America. And it is the only one in which ninety-seven per cent of the population is of European extraction or birth.

The factors that have made Argentina what it is today have been many and varied, but its circumstances of geography and contrasting climates have been responsible in no small measure for its ofttimes tragic history.

Favorable climate made the lush pampas; an unfavorable climate forced the artificial development of the dry western areas; tropical conditions created the northern forests, and the chill Antarctic winds determined the fate of Patagonia. Three of these dissimilar regions developed a diversity of interests among the settlers that retarded the development of the country as an economic and political unit for many a score of years.

In the days when it seemed that this back door to Peru might prove a quicker road to riches than the bloody trail along the Andes that Pizarro had carved, nobody took much interest in the land itself. The level pampas north and west of the Rio de la Plata, those endless seas of tall grass ranging far beyond the horizon, were merely the homes of the wild guanacos and rheas and the even wilder Indians who hunted them.

With the rich black soil seven to eleven feet thick in many places, the pampas extended for hundreds of miles, flat and unbroken, with never a stone to turn a plough. Today, as then, the level surface discourages the formation of permanent rivers, and where the soil is shallow the rainwater collects in pools that are of great value in grazing stock.

The mildness of the climate, and the distribution and quantity of rainfall, encourage the prolific growth of the pampa grasses. This rainfall averages twenty inches a year in the west to forty inches in the east, and the growing season varies from three hundred days a year in the north to a hundred and forty days in the south.

These are some of the factors that were to make the pampas the finest agricultural and stock-raising regions in the world. But in those early times no man could have foreseen that those millions of acres of grasslands would one day become the source of far greater riches than any he could hope to secure by battling death and pestilence along the 1300-mile jungle trail from the Plata River to Potosí.

Show-window of a Nation

Nor could any one of those single-minded treasure hunters have envisioned the miracle city that was to rear itself out of the mud of that river bank on the very spot where Pedro de Mendoza had put up his miserable shacks, christening them The City of Our Lady of Fair Winds (*La Ciudad de Nuestra Señora de Buenos Aires*) in 1535. But there it is today, and there, too, are more than three and a half millions of the mixed-blooded descendants of Indian and Spaniard and of European nationals who make up Argentina's twenty-million population.

Most of the pure-blooded Indians are gone. But there are the pampas, the interior provinces with their scattered towns, and the City of Buenos Aires, each as utterly unalike the other as the peoples who inhabit them.

In this youngest and most important of South American countries, the three thousand families who, until recent years, owned practically all of its sixty-million acres of cultivated lands and grazing areas, created for themselves a capital city that today combines the glamor of Paris and old Vienna with the metropolitan sophistication and uproar of a New York or Chicago. The splendid buildings, the lovely tree-lined streets, the beautiful parks, plazas, and government offices; the mile after mile of modern docks and grain elevators, all give the impression that this is the metropolis of a vastly wealthy industrial country instead of the show window of a nation of gentlemen farmers.

There are other important cities in the country—Rosario, Córdoba, LaPlata, etc.—but it is Buenos Aires that represents the great wealth of Argentina. And the contrast between its magnificence and the drabness of the habitations of the people who produce that wealth, on farms and ranches they do not own, is almost past belief. Yet in the light of history this is a logical development in a country no one wanted and few knew what to do with when it was handed to them. It is a natural result of the widely varying origins and education of its people—the lowly Indians, the Spanish and Italian workers, the better-class Europeans and their descendants; of the vast distances, the isolation of its populated areas, and the feudal system of land ownership and peonage, remnants of which persist to this day.

Porteños versus *Criollos*

Perhaps not so difficult for the outsider to understand is the deep and long-existing antagonism between the people of Buenos Aires and those of the interior—a difference that still makes itself felt in the attitude of the *porteños*, as the citizens of Buenos Aires call themselves, toward the *criollos* who live in the rest of Argentina. It is this difference and lack of cooperation between the two that was responsible for the slow development of the country in the early days, culminating in the years of anarchy that followed the achievement of independence in 1816.

The people of the capital are different from those of the hinterland, as they always have been, in origin, temperament, and outlook. And their attitude toward the rest of the country for long merely reflected the attitude of Spain toward the colony as a whole. The Spanish Crown regarded all its American colonies as existing solely for the benefit of the mother country, and enacted stringent laws to remind them of the fact.

Buenos Aires in those days being in the hands of pure-blooded Spaniards, far superior in their own minds to the adventurers who had established the settlements and opened up the country at the cost of their lives, considered themselves representatives of a superior civilization. Such an attitude, offensive to normal people at any time, aroused the resentment of the criollos who accordingly opposed them upon every possible occasion. The criollos could not forget that they, too, were white and, being bred and born in the land, looked upon themselves as the only true Argentinians. That they had good grounds for their stand is evident from their history.

As we saw earlier, in conquest times the northern forests were populated by amiable Guaraní Indians and the plains by the much less friendly Pampas tribe. From those early days many a Guaraní mother bore a stalwart Spanish son, or a golden-skinned daughter to become the lady of a Don. The Pampas Indians, however, wanted none of that. They had their horses, game was plentiful, and they valued their liberty and way of life above all else. Hence while the Guaranís were mothering a new and virile race, the Pampas preferred to take their chances either of being pushed farther and farther into Patagonia or exterminated. And extermination was eventually their fate.

But in the early days the Pampas Indians were left pretty much alone unless they attacked the white men—which they did on every possible occasion. In addition to the Guaranís and Pampas there was at this time a much more advanced culture occupying the eastern slopes of the Andes in territory that is now a part of Argentina. This was the Huarapos tribe, subjects of the Incas, who had constructed extensive irrigation systems, turning large, arid areas into highly productive agricultural lands.

In the valleys and on the plains of the Andean foothills, the Huarapos were producing large quantities of potatoes, maize, and wheat long before the Spaniards came. Since this area was far south of the Potosí region which was the goal of the Spaniards coming in from the Atlantic side of the Continent, it escaped their unwelcome attentions entirely. When these highly productive oases were finally discovered it was by conquistadors from the Chilean side of the Andes who descended into Argentina to contest the rights of an earlier expedition from Lima.

As a result of this dispute between the Spaniards of Chile and those of Peru, a town called Santiago del Estero was founded by the Chileans. This was the first town to be established in Argentina proper. The controversy was settled by the King of Spain giving this territory to the Peruvian viceroy who thereupon founded the town of Tucumán as capital of that region in 1565.

Paraguay River Settlements

Later in the Sixteenth Century the necessity for keeping the Portuguese out of the River Plata territory, plus the desirability of establishing bases from which raids could be made on Incan outposts, led to the founding of settlements in the Paraguay River region. Headquarters for the River Plata conquistadors was Asunción, now the modern capital of Paraguay. Soon the difficulties of conducting these expeditions, and the uncertainty of results made it imperative that the Spaniards seek some more dependable means of obtaining the necessities of life.

Food was a problem with the Spaniards even more than it had been with the Indians. There was little that the aboriginals could do to supply the conquistadors with the kinds of food they needed, or indeed any food at all. In the end it became obvious that the Spaniards would have to make their own arrangements for food supplies if they were not to starve to death. This they did by clearing land and establishing farms, making use of Indian labor.

At this time all new colonists came to Asunción overland from Santa Catharina on the Brazilian coast, a long and hazardous journey. Few ships from Spain would even attempt the tortuous voyage up the rivers from the Atlantic to Paraguay. The necessity for a convenient port and supply base on the Atlantic had long been evident, but the ferocity of the Indians in the lower River Plata region had always discouraged the colonists from attempting to re-establish Buenos Aires which the savages had forced them to abandon almost as soon as it was begun. As a compromise they founded, in 1573, the town of Santa Fé de Vera Cruz (present-day Santa Fé) near the junction of the Paraná with the Salado River. This was more-or-less safe territory, and formed a useful base for the subsequent jump to Buenos Aires.

Refounding of Buenos Aires

By 1580 there was a sufficient number of Spanish-Indian mestizos in Santa Fé to form a protective garrison for a settlement farther down the River Plata. Accordingly, two hundred Guaraní Indian families, guarded by about three score mestizos mounted on horses (Argentina's first gauchos) moved to the site of Buenos Aires under the command of Juan de Garay and ten other Spaniards.

On the banks of a small creek, the Riachuelo, they

built a stockade for themselves and their large supply of horses, cows, and sheep. Soon the land around the new settlement was parcelled out among the Spaniards in sizable farms and ranches which the Indians worked. The Spaniards quickly discovered that their wild Indian neighbors, the Pampas, were as warlike as ever and resented their presence on the pampa which was now the home range of thousands of wild horses and cattle. But the mounted men of the garrison, with their speedy horses and their uncanny skill with the boleadoras, were more than a match for the Indians.

This was territory made to order for the horseman. These hard-riding, tough half-breeds—who had not yet acquired the disparaging cognomen of gaucho—had no interest in farming. All they wanted out of life was a horse and a rope and a knife and freedom to roam the pampa. Thanks to them, within three years of the founding of the town, shiploads of hides and tallow were on their way to Spain. And so was born the trade in animal products that was to become the basic source of Argentina's wealth.

Unfortunately for the white men who had begun to scent riches in the carcasses of steers and horses, their government still preferred gold and silver. In order to discourage the export of anything else, and to maintain a check on everything sent from the Indies to Spain, all shipments by sea from the east coast were prohibited in 1599.

The Smugglers

From the time of the invasion of Peru, Spain had been sending two fleets a year under convoy to the Caribbean.

These brought supplies and took back treasure, much to the delight and profit of pirates and units of the English Navy who preyed upon them. Therefore, everything from Peru and Argentina had to be shipped through Lima and across the isthmus of Panama. Obviously, this was a tremendous hardship for the Spanish in Paraguay and the River Plata territory and, as might have been expected, smuggling began on a large scale. Cattle, hides, grain, and small quantities of silver, formed an increasingly valuable export trade. Furthermore, in 1608, the shipment of salted beef to Cuba and Brazil was begun, and horsehair was added to the list of commodities that found a ready market in Europe.

Unable to divert their warships from the Caribbean to check this flow of contraband, the Spanish Crown finally, in 1617, decided to make the territory southeast of Paraguay into the separate Province of Buenos Aires, under a resident Governor. Thereafter a succession of governors came and went, but the smuggling continued unabated. The white men, growing rich, established one town after another at strategic points from which they could supervise the trade that the Indians and their half-breed sons were creating for them.

The Settling of Argentina

By this time the western part of the country had long been settled by Spaniards from Chile and Peru. The Incas had developed this agricultural section by irrigating the arid areas in order to supply the mining parts of Bolivia with food. This source of food became even more important after the arrival of the Spaniards when the production of the mines was stepped up through the use of forced labor, and the conquistadors had to be fed as well as the Indians. The Spaniards imported cattle and the region was soon supplying them with dairy products and meat. To provide grazing for the cattle, the occupied area was extended to include a number of scattered oases, and this led to the establishment of several more centers of population.

In a comparatively short time this region became so productive that there was a surplus of products for export to Spain via Lima. Farther to the south, the settlement established by Chile in the Mendoza territory was given over to agriculture, but since there was no outside market for these products it did not, for a long time, advance beyond subsistence farming.

These two areas, nevertheless, had a number of things in common. For one, they were both governed from Lima and had no direct contact with Spain. They were both remote from Buenos Aires, and their populations were composed of domesticated Indians. The number of pure-blooded Indians shrank rapidly as more and more of the women bore children to Spanish fathers. But always there were enough Indians to maintain the native way of life, and the mestizo offspring, more often than not, were more Indian in their ideas and outlook than they were Spanish. As a result, both Indians and mestizos lived together on a basis of equality and in more or less primitive style, with one paramount interest—the soil.

As for the Spaniards themselves, they seem to have felt that their loyalties lay more in the direction of Peru than Buenos Aires and the eastern territories governed directly from Spain. This was an important factor in their attitude toward Buenos Aires of which they were as independent as if it had been another colony.

From all of this it will be seen that during the Seventeenth Century a great change had taken place in the relationship between the Spaniards and the Indians. The few Indians and the great many more mestizos were now the producers of the country's wealth on a significant scale, and therefore had to be encouraged rather than repressed. This attitude was further stimulated by the fact that an entirely new race was springing up in each of the several occupied regions.

In the Andean foothills the more advanced cultures were isolated from their neighbors by the Andean peaks on the West and arid terrain to the East. But the Indians remembered their disciplined existence under the Incas, and their tradition of dependence set them apart from the wild and independent Indians of the forests and pampas whom fate had marked for extermination. With the coming of the Spaniards, the more civilized Indians had merely changed masters and remained docile and content. This binding force encouraged their development as a unit both socially and politically. The Spaniards, on the other hand, maintained themselves as overlords and aristocrats, and dwelt apart in their towns.

On the pampas, and on the east coast, conditions were entirely different. The eastern area, which included the town of Buenos Aires, was governed directly from Spain. Originally it was composed of the Adelantazgo of Rio de la Plata. In 1617 this had been divided into the Provinces of Paraguay and Rio de la Plata. The latter included the *Banda Oriental* on the north side of the river, which later became the independent country of Uruguay. For the time being, however, the territory of Buenos Aires became the commercial and political center of an area that included the vast pampas, the forests, and the grasslands, extending on both sides of the River Plata from the Atlantic to Bolivia in the north, and the borders of the western territories.

By the year 1600, the people inhabiting this territory were largely a mixture of Spanish and Indian. Most of those Indians in the Paraguay area were put to work growing grain and breeding cattle for the Europeans. Those farther south roamed the plains, providing the horse and cattle products with which the contraband trade through Buenos Aires was built up.

Though religion did not play as important a role in early colonial Argentina as it did in many other South American countries, it cannot go unnoticed. The River Plata area was opened up on a much smaller scale than was Peru. Therefore no great numbers of priests accompanied the soldiers. Under an arrangement known as the encomienda system, the conquistadors were allowed to seize and enslave as many Indians as they sought fit, and a great many cruelties were perpetrated as a consequence.

The Jesuits Go into Business

In 1586, the Adelantado then in office—Vera y Aragon—recognized the evil, but the only way he could combat it was to permit religious orders to establish missions. At his invitation, Franciscan missionaries settled in Tucumán, and three Jesuit priests—a Spaniard, a Scotsman, and a Portuguese—moved into Paraguay. In the course of the years the Jesuits erected missions and a college. Later they were given the territory of Guayra, and a concession which forbade anyone enslaving or otherwise mistreating any Guaraní Indians belonging to the Jesuit mission.

Molested by the inhabitants of a Brazilian border town, the missions were forced to move south to a territory that even today is called Misiones. Here they put up houses for the Indians, erected schools, and organized small farms. The Indians were taught a number of useful trades such as tanning, weaving, and carpentry.

In this way the missionaries made each settlement practically self-supporting, even to the extent of selling their products outside the missions. The male Indians were taught the use of arms so that they could protect the missions from attack, and these miniature armies were, on more than one occasion, borrowed by the provincial or national governments to help combat uprisings or invasions.

Maté, cotton, and tobacco were grown and the missions became wealthy, extending their control from the Indians to the Spanish and mestizo citizens within their domain. Their trading activities developed into outright commercial competition with the rest of the country, and, being immune to taxes, they enjoyed an unfair advantage. They also indulged in contraband trade. The Indians the missions protected became virtually slaves, and what little benefit they derived from their labors was taken from them in the form of forced contributions for ecclesiastical benefits.

Eventually the Jesuits became so powerful that they had great influence in the provincial and territorial governments. So superior did they feel themselves that they looked upon all other religious orders with contempt, thereby quite naturally arousing hatred. They were finally expelled in 1767 as a result of public protests in Spain and elsewhere, and the indignation of the Spanish Government at their interference with negotiations between Spain and Portugal regarding colonial affairs.

The net result of the Jesuits' activities was to hasten the commercial development of the country to some degree, and to give some scores of thousands of Indians a taste for a more civilized existence. Undoubtedly it made large numbers of them politically conscious, and contributed to the spirit of independence that proved so strong a factor in the struggle between the provinces and localities for the preservation of their individual autonomies.

Origin of the Gauchos

It was on these grassy plains with their vast herds of wild animals that an entirely new race of men was bred—those horse-riding hunters and cowboys of mixed origin, the gauchos. In those days of unfenced, limitless ranges, the gauchos roamed great distances. Sleeping on the ground with the sky for a tent, many of them neither needed nor wanted permanent homes. Those who had settled down were content with adobe shacks under sod roofs, and a woman to do all the work that did not call for riding.

In strange contrast with the gauchos were the Spanish organizers of the contraband trade, the politicians bent on organizing the country, the treasure hunters, the speculators, and their Indian and metizo servants, together with the farmers in and around Buenos Aires.

These, then, were the peoples who inhabited the four new Provinces—Paraguay and Buenos Aires in the east; Tucumán and Cuyo in the west—and set a pattern for the country's growth. Of the three groups, the most active and for a long time the most important, were the gauchos. These half-wild horsemen, a law unto themselves, became the great force that developed Argentina and took a leading part in establishing its independence. Their origin therefore calls for some study.

Conquistadors and Concubines

For a century or more, as we have seen, conquistadors roamed the area from the mouth of the River Plata to the borders of Bolivia. And wherever they went they took to themselves the brown-skinned women, principally of the Guaraní tribe. Few, if any, limited themselves to one or two women. For example, in the early days of Asunción, the small group of colonists under Domingo Martínez de Irala had no fewer than seven hundred Indian girls at their service. When they tired of one woman they simply took another.

The expeditions conducted by the Spaniards with the help of their Indian friends resulted in large numbers of the Indians being killed by enemy tribesmen through whose territory they were forced to pass. These two simple facts, together with a number of more abstruse ones were responsible for the decrease in the number of male Indians and the ever-increasing number of mestizo children born.

As time went on and these children of mixed blood grew up, the females among them were in great demand by the white men as concubines and, in rare instances, as wives. Mestizo men also married mestizo women, and their daughters married or consorted with white men. The net result of this continuous intermixture of the races was the rapid evolution of individuals with less and less of the characteristics of the Indian and more of those of the white man. In the end they came to be classed as whites and they, as well as the American-born Spaniards, were called criollos, a designation they bear to this day.

An important fact which must not be overlooked in this connection is that not all of the conquistadors were Spaniards. A great many free-lance adventurers of Portuguese, German, Italian, and even Arab descent, joined the Spaniards on their expeditions, particularly as members of the lower ranks.

Beginnings of a New Race

In the new white race that developed from this continuous cross-breeding, little remained of the characteristics of either of the parent races after five generations or more. This new individual was the parent stock of the gaucho, the true Argentinian, loving the soil and freedom, living in a wide, wild world of his own, and acknowledging no man as his master. Of medium height, the grown man was bent and bowlegged from a life in the saddle, his olive skin tanned almost to blackness. Black eyed, and often bearded, he was the essence of masculinity—a picture of physical vigor and wiry, muscular strength. Mounted on his horse, galloping across the pampa, poncho flying and boleadoras whirling, he was the embodiment of all the masculine traits of which poets sing and that women adore.

His was no planned life. When he was hungry or in need of hides to trade for silver ornaments for his horse, he killed as many cattle as the situation required, skinned them, and trotted off to town leaving the carcasses to the vultures or to rot in the sun. The gaucho was picturesque. He was also primitive, ignorant, and in our eyes cruel, yet his country owes him a great debt. In many ways the history of the gaucho is the history of Argentina.

In time there were many thousands of these men roaming the pampas, often singly, at times in groups—especially when there were Pampas Indians to be fought. Little by little the gauchos extended their hunting grounds, driving southward the Indians they did not exterminate. Their uncivilized mode of living, and their attitude toward the people of the towns they despised, earned for them the disgust of the Spaniards who looked upon them as barbarians and outlaws. Even the name Gaucho was originally a term of contempt. But this attitude was to turn to one of admiration and gratitude when the day came for the battle for independence.

Originally, much of the land outside the pampas, in and around the settlements, had been apportioned to the conquistadors according to their rank and importance. Their sons acquired more land as the country was opened up through the gradual extinction of the Indian populations. As it became more and more evident that the riches of Argentina lay in its soil, new arrivals from Spain took up land either by grant from the Spanish Crown or by purchase. Most of these settled in Buenos Aires, a shabby town of adobe huts and muddy streets, the yellow river on one side and wide fields of grain on the other. Those of the new white race who had stuck to the towns and acquired wealth from trade with their gaucho brethren also were permitted to possess land. Out of the ranks of these criollos began to arise the new aristocracy of Argentina.

As civilization encroached on the pampas, the land owners established homes on their *estancias*. The gauchos, oblingingly pushing the savage Indians before them, moved farther into the wilderness.

The Gaucho Caudillos

Always between the estancias and the Indians, the gauchos were forced to band together in large groups for mutual protection. Out of this necessity came the leaders of the gauchos, the *caudillos* (chiefs) who took command of their respective groups during Indian raids. As a natural result, each of these caudillos became a power in his locality and did not hesitate to use that power for political ends. In their favor was the fact that centers of population were widespread and isolated, with no means of direct, safe, or speedy communication between them. The inevitable outcome was the establishment of strong local governments, independent, and jealous of outside interference.

Meanwhile the gaucho preferred a life of excitement to gold, and although he traded with the porteños he still clung to his independence. As time went on, however, the need for gauchos diminished. When the cattle ranges were fenced off, making it possible to plant wheat over vast areas, there was more call for farm labor and less for horsemen. Some of the gauchos became "*gauchos pastores*" (pasture herdsmen) and tilled the fields; others drifted into the towns and became simple peons. Eventually their descendants came to constitute the huge reservoir of general labor that built up the population of the cities, though many still clung to the land and eked out a miserable existence as share-croppers. But before that day arrived the people of the hinterland, the gauchos and criollos had developed such an antipathy to the Spanish-born, the land-owners and the exporters who lived in Buenos Aires, that much blood was shed before they became reconciled and united under a federal government.

In attempting to understand how the modern country developed from these unpromising beginnings it is helpful to delve a little into the political history of the country before the day of independence which saw the birth of three nations where there had been but one.

In the beginning the development of the rich pampa region was retarded by the difficulties of sending livestock products and agricultural commodities over to the Pacific for export to Spain. Buenos Aires was the only logical outlet, and since shipping direct to Spain was forbidden there was no recourse but smuggling. In this the Argentinians had the full cooperation of those European countries that were far from friendly toward Spain. Under these conditions, however, Buenos Aires could make little headway until 1776 when the port was legally opened to commerce with Spain.

Even then prosperity was still a long way off. Spain soon became so preoccupied with conducting a war against Napoleon that she had little chance to develop trade with the colony. When the English joined the French in sweeping the Spanish ships from the seas, the situation of the colony became precarious.

The Wave of Independence

An English warship attacked and took Buenos Aires in 1806, but an army of gauchos recaptured the city, much to their own surprise. Finding themselves quite capable of defending their country from a foreign power, the criollos, with the example of the United States of North America before them, began to think of independence. When they were again attacked by the English in the following year they achieved another great victory. Convinced of their military might, it needed only a tyrannical act on the part of the Spanish king, Ferdinand VII, to drive the criollos into action.

The extraordinary pitch to which hatred of Spain had risen during the revolutionary war was demonstrated by the action of the provisional government which, in 1815, offered Argentina to Great Britain as a self-governing colony. With the declaration of independence, which was finally achieved in 1816, a wave of enthusiasm for the new freedom swept across the pampas. But while it rid the colony of oppression from Spain it did not bring peace and prosperity. The wide rift between Buenos Aires and the rest of the country became a seemingly unbridgeable chasm. The authorities in Buenos Aires set themselves up as rulers of the whole country, and thereby launched a series of bloody revolts. Both Paraguay and Uruguay became separate countries, and the rest of the provinces battled one another for supremacy. Many of them were split by factions, each seeking to establish control of their province and of the nation, and none of them was willing to be governed by any other.

During the next fifty years this struggle gradually emerged as a contest between the city and the country—

the *campo*—or camp, as it is now called. Two major political parties were formed, the Federalistas and the Unitarios. The Federalistas wanted a federal republic, giving the provinces all the privileges of independent states. The Unitarios fought for a centralized government operating from Buenos Aires.

Evolution of the Modern State

Several new, independent provinces were formed, and each struggling for supremacy added to the general confusion. Various governmental expedients were tried out before the first general Congress was formed in Buenos Aires in 1825. In 1826, this Congress appointed, as first constitutional President, Bernardino Rivadavia who had served in the various governments since 1812.

Rivadavia was a businessman who developed into a statesman. He organized the police and postal systems, the universities and schools; he separated the Church from the State, and founded the nation's legal system. He abolished slavery (which had never been important), and the discrimination against foreigners in trade. He established a uniform system of currency, and put the national treasury on a sound basis. In the Congress of 1825 his efforts at establishing national unity were blocked by the provincial caudillos, and he was forced to leave the country. In his absence the Congress, like a ship without a rudder, got nowhere. Unable to agree on a Constitution, they floundered into a war with Brazil over the status of Uruguay which, once an Argentine Province, wanted to be entirely independent of both Argentina and Brazil.

In 1826 the Congress recalled Rivadavia, made him

President, and agreed on a Constitution that was at once rejected by the Provincials. By successfully concluding the war with Brazil, Rivadavia freed Uruguay, but he still could not obtain the support of the provinces and finally was forced to retire.

The next two presidents did not last long. One was murdered and the other driven out of the country, in 1829, to make way for a Federalist dictator who had long been the "boss of Buenos Aires,"—Juan Manuel de Rosas. This ruthless tyrant ruled Argentina for the next twenty-four years.

Tall and powerfully built, de Rosas in his youth had managed his father's huge cattle ranch, and had become an even more skilled and daring horseman than the gauchos who worked for him. Naturally they idolized him. When he went into the cattle business for himself, de Rosas organized the gauchos and put them in scarlet jackets. These were his storm troops, his private militia which he employed to discourage his enemies—and once to quell a political uprising in Buenos Aires. Soon after that incident he became leader of the Federalistas, and was elected Governor of the Province of Buenos Aires.

In 1829, de Rosas took over the Presidency of the Argentine Confederation. The Unitarios fled to Uruguay, and de Rosas turned his attention to the Indians of the pampas, driving south to Patagonia those he did not slaughter. In this way he freed the pampas, and added vast areas of grazing lands to be divided among the influential Spanish families. Intensely nationalistic and belligerent, de Rosas picked quarrels with both Bolivia and Uruguay. He fought the French who blockaded Buenos Aires, and the English who seized the Falkland Islands. And with his red-jacketed gauchos he finally compelled the provinces to submit to government, or rather dictation, from Buenos Aires.

Finally, in 1852, de Rosas was dislodged by another Federalista, the despotic governor Urquiza of the Province of Entre Rios. It was now the turn of the porteños to refuse to have anything to do with a government elected by the criollos, and they seceded from the confederation. Undaunted, Urquiza set up his government at Paraná and for seven years ruled without them.

Even under these conditions the country was still far from peaceful. Civil strife and armed revolts were frequent during the next fifty years. Immigrants, encouraged now that Spanish control had been abolished, found little to attract them. Most of the land was in the hands of the large landowners and there were few opportunities for the small farmer. Sheep had been imported as early as 1825, but the trade in animal products grew slowly. In over half a century—from 1800 to 1852—the population had only expanded from 900,000 to 1,200,000. Poor roads and communications militated against any large-scale social or economic development, and limited the sources of trade.

Under Urquiza the first federal constitution acceptable to all parties was adopted, and organized attempts made to revive a country stagnant after years of unrest. Starting in 1850, a series of forts was established to guard the settled area from attacks by savage Indians, both north and south of Buenos Aires. By 1854 most of the navigable waters had been opened to trade and a beginning made in the construction of railways connecting Buenos Aires with important centers. But it took twenty-five years to extend them to the margins of the pampa and connect the western centers with salt-water ports.

The Rise of the Middle Classes

Not till 1860 did the city join the provinces in electing a president acceptable to both. This was President Bartholomé Mítre who launched Argentina as a modern state. During this time the tide of emigration began to flow, an influx that was to change the entire character of the Argentinian population. Thousands of English, Scottish, and Irish sheep and cattle herders were followed by swarms of Italians and other Southern Europeans. From 1800 to 1850, the population of the United States of North America had jumped from five millions to twenty-three millions, and by 1865, the U.S.A. was supplying foreign markets that Argentina could very well have used. With the advent of our Civil War much of this market became available to Argentina which was then in a much better position to take advantage of the opportunity offered. The market generally was also expanding due to the industrialization of Europe.

In 1877, the whole export trade of Argentina was revolutionized by the introduction of refrigeration. This period also marked the widespread acquisition of agricultural machinery, including mechanical pumps and windmills. The pastures were fenced off, better breeding stock was introduced, and richer feed, such as alfalfa, planted. Quality cattle production under controlled conditions replaced the haphazard methods that left everything to Nature and the gauchos. The herds became bigger and better, and slaughtering and freezing plants were constructed so that frozen and chilled meats could be shipped in place of live cattle or salted beef.

The sheep industry, which spread over enormous areas throughout Patagonia, for the first time made use of the

1. Charcoal is the indispensable domestic fuel throughout most of South America. In the Chaco forests of Argentina it is made from these huge mounds of wood made airtight by a thick coating of clay. The hollow log in the foreground serves as a tank to hold water used in making the clay mud.

2. This sky-view of Buenos Aires, Argentina, is dominated by the Atlas Building, the tallest edifice in South America.

3. (*right*) Products from around the world can be found in this fashionable shopping district of Buenos Aires, Argentina—the Callé Florida.

4. (*below*) As the crowds in this view indicate, Bristol Beach at Mar del Plata is Argentina's most popular seaside resort.

5. (*top, opposite page*) One of Argentina's famed beauty spots (which it shares with Brazil), the Iguazú Falls. Their power-producing potential is enormous.

6. (*bottom, opposite page*) Argentine Gauchos demonstrate their prowess in a steer-roping contest.

7. (*top of page, left*) The Casa Rosada, Buenos Aires, Argentina, home of the presidents.

8. (*top of page, right*) The Plaza Congreso, Buenos Aires, Argentina. The government building adds beauty to a stately city in a land grown rich on cattle instead of found gold.

9. (*below*) A subtropical panorama in Uruguay—Montevideo's outskirts dotted with white buildings and palm trees under a midday sun, a peaceful scene befitting a country where the extremes of wealth and poverty are not as great as in other countries.

10. (*top, opposite page*) One of the rapidly vanishing back country settlements in Uruguay which the government is endeavoring to transform into modern communities through education and the creation of work opportunities.

11. (*center, opposite page*) Downtown Montevideo, capital of Uruguay, is replete with parks, plazas, trees and beautiful buildings, reflecting a leisurely Latin life.

12. (*bottom, opposite page*) Independence Plaza marks the center of Montevideo.

13. (*below*) Gardening and husbandry form one of the fifty community projects launched by the government of Paraguay to teach the natives a wide range of skills as part of their general education.

Asunción, the capital of Paraguay, has its share of fine Spanish architecture.

14. (*top*) Colonial architecture
15. (*right*) Revolutionary architecture
16. (*below*) Modern architecture

whole carcasses instead of just the wool and sometimes the fat of the animals. Refrigerated railroad cars and ships made possible the transport of all these things to distant countries. Meanwhile, with the cattle fenced in, it was possible to plant large areas with wheat, corn, and other cereals. The country was transformed. From the pampa came beef, mutton, wool, linseed oil, wheat, oats, and corn for human consumption. From the Mesopotamia District (Entre Rios, Corrientes, and Misiones) came mutton, beef, and *yerba maté* (Paraguayan tea); the low Chaco plains supplied cotton and quebracho, the world's most important source of tannin extract used in making leather. The irrigated areas of the dry west grew sugar cane and supported vineyards that produced excellent wines. There, also, large numbers of goats were raised. In Patagonia oil was discovered to supplement the products of the sheep ranches. And in all these activities the great influx of immigrants was a vital factor.

Today there are two-and-a-half times as many cattle in Argentina as there are human beings, and almost as many sheep. This tremendous growth of products and population during the nineteenth century and early part of the twentieth, brought about changes in the people as well as the land. In the Argentina of today there is a total population of about nineteen and a half millions. Almost a fifth of that number live in Buenos Aires which handles three quarters of the country's foreign commerce. About one third of these people are foreign-born or second-generation Italian, Spanish, French, Russian, Turkish, and German. The gaucho population has shrunk to less than a quarter of a million and the civilized Indians to forty thousand or less.

A vast majority of the more recent immigrants go to swell Argentina's large and growing, comfortable middle class. The Italian immigrants in particular, with their latin origin and the ease with which they master the Spanish language, have proved readily assimilable. Quite a few of these first- or second-generation Argentinians have accumulated wealth, and some have held important positions in both provincial and national governments.

A contributing factor in this assimilation process is undoubtedly the fact that education is compulsory and the schools modern. Argentina actually has about the lowest percentage of illiterates in South America—somewhere between seven and ten per cent.

Since Argentina has little in the way of metals, especially iron, and since it has no coal and comparatively little oil, it has not been possible to develop much in the way of heavy industry. In the larger cities, and in and around Buenos Aires, some essential industries have been developed, ranging from the production and processing of foods, beverages, and tobacco, to the manufacturing of machines and vehicles. These, naturally, have attracted to the urban areas large numbers of workers. But another reason for the tendency of the population to concentrate in the towns is the lack of small farms and ranches, and the difficulties encountered in operating those that are available. For some years the government has recognized this and encouraged banks to extend loans to small farmers *(chacareros)* to finance improvements, seed and fertilizer, and equipment. They have also encouraged colonization by extending electrification, and promoting the increase in building and improvement of standards in rural housing.

The country is nominally Roman Catholic in religion

and the President must subscribe to that faith. In practice, a large proportion of the male population, particularly among the educated classes, seem to look upon organized religion as a social force to which they are happy to see their women folk contribute, but with which they are not otherwise greatly concerned. The Roman Catholic Church actually has less authority in Argentina than in almost any other South American country.

The Peronistas and After

In politics, the people appear to incline toward democratic ideals and institutions more strongly as the level of education rises. But first and foremost they are Argentines, proud of their political and commercial achievements, and their standing as a great power in the modern world. On the other hand, since the end of World War II, Argentina has suffered a number of economic setbacks (in common with most of South America) from which it is only slowly recovering. The election in 1946 of Colonel Juan D. Perón as President resulted in the wide restriction of liberties and some unsound economic measures whose effects have not yet been wholly overcome.

In the period from 1946 to 1955 when Perón was unseated, the nation's savings were squandered, and unrealistic industrialization plans adopted. The Provisional regime which followed had to contend with both severe economic difficulties and counter-revolutionary activities that gave rise to extreme labor unrest. The basic policy however was, and continues to be under a duly elected President, Dr. Pedro E. Aramburu, that of maintaining only so long as necessary for the economic health of the country, rigid state controls, especially of exports, with State monopolies of oil and electric power, both of which are capable of being greatly expanded.

The ratification of multilateral trade and payments agreements with eleven European countries in 1957 should contribute to the revivifying of both industry and agriculture and hasten the return to a sound economy. Meanwhile this second largest of South America's Republics has been among the first in putting into practice plans to help build a stronger South America by aiding weaker neighbors develop their own resources.

U R U G U A Y

P A R A G U A Y

CHAPTER 6

URUGUAY PARAGUAY: LANDS OF MATÉ AND QUEBRACHO

THE SMALL REPUBLICS OF URUGUAY and Paraguay are an excellent example of how far apart two countries of almost identical origin can grow. Originally, both were a part of the viceroyalty of La Plata from which Argentina was formed. Today Paraguay is somewhat less than two and a half times the area of Uruguay but has a little more than half the population. Its people are nearly all Spanish-Indian, with the Indian blood predominating, and the language is mainly Guaraní.

Uruguay, on the other hand, has a population that is almost purely European in origin, speaking Spanish, and with a very high standard of literacy. Paraguay is poor, and isolated in the interior, while Uruguay is rich and possesses the best transportation facilities, both by land and water, of any South American country.

But geography is far from being the sole determining factor in the development of these two countries. The things that made them what they are today lie far deeper than that.

Uruguay

Uruguay was originally the Banda Oriental (Eastern Border) of what was to become Argentina, but in the early days of the conquistadors it was inhabited by even more savage and warlike Indians than those of the Argentine pampa—the Charrúas.

The first few attempts by the Spaniards at establishing a foothold on the coast were driven off or the forces wiped out. In several instances towns were later built, but had to be abandoned within a year or two, and the Indians razed them. In 1603, Hernando Arias de Saavedra, the first governor of the River Plata region to be born there, led an expedition of five hundred men against the Charrúas and was ignominiously defeated.

Hernandarias, as de Saavedra was called, was one of the few to escape. Seeing that force was of little avail, he next tried guile. From Buenos Aires he shipped across the river a hundred head of cattle, and a hundred horses and mares, and turned them loose. His idea undoubtedly was that the animals would multiply, as they had done in Argentina, and when the time came to subdue the country there would be a ready-made source of wealth awaiting them. However, as it turned out, a band of priests and not an army, made the first conquest of this wild territory.

In 1618, two Franciscan fathers landed to work among the more peaceable tribes. In 1625, a Jesuit settlement was founded in the southwest. Shortly afterwards, large missions were established in the north. These were really extensions of the Jesuit organization in Paraguay. The horses and cattle introduced by Hernandarias multiplied tremendously in a short time, and the mission Indians were put to work in cattle raising and agriculture. The wild Charrúas now had turned to riding horses and eating meat, and, since this food was plentiful, they offered less resistance to the newcomers encroaching on their territory.

The wild herds in the South were so numerous that the government in Buenos Aires licensed gauchos to raid the coastal areas and collect hides. These men soon found themselves in competition with adventurers who did not bother to obtain licenses. The outlaws grew in numbers to such an extent that they were able to resist the government officers sent after them. When they could not so resist, they simply fled across the border into Brazil. The licensed gauchos, meanwhile, had established a number of small settlements along the coast and rivers.

Wars between Spain and Portugal

In 1680, the first of many struggles between Spain and Portugal for possession of the country took place. A Portuguese fleet landed a number of colonist families, and set about founding the township of Colonia do Sacramento. In order to expel these intruders, the governor of Buenos Aires borrowed 3,000 armed Indians from the Jesuits. With these mercenaries and three hundred Spaniards he took the Portuguese as prisoners. He was, no doubt, much embarrassed when, a mere year later, Carlos II of Spain signed a treaty with Portugal, giving Colonia back to that country.

At this time the Indians began to discover that they, too, could do a good business in hides and dried meat. And, like their more civilized brothers, the more business they did the more greedy they became. In 1702 it seemed necessary for the white man to wage war on the savages, and many tribes were entirely wiped out.

In Portuguese hands, the port of Colonia quickly became the center of contraband trade with the closed port of Buenos Aires. This annoyed Philip V of Spain who ordered it recaptured. It took four thousand Indians, two thousand Spanish troops, and a six-month's siege to force the garrison to flee. After all of this, King Philip, in 1713, ceded the town back to the Portuguese in the Treaty of Utrecht. But the Governor of Buenos Aires, who did not like the idea at all, seized on a technicality to limit Portuguese possession to the distance of a cannon shot from the center of town.

At this time, Negro slaves were brought into the River Plata region, as a part of a campaign on the part of the clergy to release Indians from slavery. Some of the Negroes were landed in the Banda Oriental, although the Spanish inhabitants were not much interested in them. However, since the Spaniards in this section had not made slaves of the Indians, they soon found that the extra labor supply was welcome, and the country benefited. But the troubles of the colonists were not over!

At the end of 1723, the Portuguese sent 300 soldiers on four ships from Rio de Janeiro, Brazil, to establish a base for the conquest of Uruguay. They landed at a point where the capital city, Montevideo, now stands. They came to terms with the local Indians, supplied them with arms, and set about forming a settlement. Once more the governor of Buenos Aires rushed to dispossess them. When the Portuguese learned of the formidable size of the attacking force, they fled to the North.

To prevent a repetition of the incident, the governor

constructed fortifications, garrisoned the place with a hundred Spanish troops and a thousand Indian auxiliaries. On December 24th, 1726, he sent seven families over from Buenos Aires to formally found the city of Montevideo. Shortly afterwards, twenty families were brought from the Canary Islands to swell the population.

In order to encourage settlement in the Banda Oriental, immigrants were offered free transportation from Buenos Aires, a plot of land, free transport of building materials, and land in the camp. Each was given 200 cattle, 100 sheep, and all the necessary tools and implements to operate a farm. Furthermore, they were excused from paying taxes until they were well established.

Two years after the founding of Montevideo thirty more families were imported from the Canaries and Galicia (a province of north-western Spain). At the end of 1728, Montevideo could boast of 200 citizens, 400 soldiers, and 1,000 Indian auxiliaries. But in 1730 it was on the point of being wiped out by an uprising of the Charrúas. More than one hundred of the soldiers were killed, and the Indians were only prevented from murdering the settlers and razing the town by the intervention of a Jesuit priest, Padre Heran.

Right after this, the Portuguese invaded the country from the North, overrunning the district of Rio Grande. A treaty signed in 1750, traded to the Portuguese both Rio Grande and the Jesuit Missions district for the town of Colonia. The Jesuits and most of the Indians were forced to seek a new place to settle. Those Indians who did not go with them were practically wiped out in a short time, the survivors being transported to Maldonado where they founded the present town.

In order to forestall further conquest by infiltration,

the Governor, Ceballos, had all the Portuguese settlers along the East coast moved to a settlement near Maldonado. When the Jesuits were expelled in 1767, the Indians they abandoned wandered west and south. Twelve families of them founded the western town of Paysandu, and several others later on. The rest of the Indians settled in the Montevideo and Maldonado areas and occupied themselves as farm workers.

It was not till 1774 that the Portuguese again attempted invasions, first from the North and then from the East. These incursions repulsed, they returned in 1776, and captured the town of San Pedro and surrounding territory. Ceballos, who was in Spain at the time, being made first Viceroy, left Cadiz with a powerful fleet and 9,000 troops, to clear the Portuguese out of Banda Oriental once and for all.

The island of Santa Catalina and Colonia were quickly seized. To make Colonia less of a prize, Ceballos destroyed its fortifications and razed its largest houses. Then he set out to plant the flag of Spain once more in Rio Grande. Again his plans were thwarted by news of an ill-timed treaty which reserved the mines of Colonia to Spain but turned over the island of Santa Catalina and most of Rio Grande to Portugal.

British Occupation

In the following period of peace, many more families immigrated from Galicia and the Canary Islands, and a score of towns were founded. Montevideo itself had a population of nearly 7,000 Spaniards, 1,400 Negro slaves,

500 liberated Negroes, and 715 mestizos and Indians. Within a few years, large numbers of black slaves were added to the population. One more Brazilian raid marked the turn of the century, and in 1806 it was the turn of the British to invade the country in the course of their war against Spain.

For a time the British occupied Montevideo, Maldonado, Colonia and a number of smaller towns. (This was the period during which they also captured Buenos Aires.) A large number of British business organizations took advantage of the occupation, and built up commercial relations with the citizens of the Banda Oriental. When they left it was in an atmosphere of mutual good will, presumably arising from the colonists' appreciation of the comparatively beneficial British trading laws and methods. At any rate, this brief association was of lasting benefit to the country and foreshadowed the close cooperation and friendship with the British which was to characterize the foreign relations of Uruguay in the years to come.

This was the time when the rest of the Viceroyalty of La Plata (now Argentina, Paraguay, and part of Bolivia) was preparing to throw off the yoke of Spain and strike for independence. But in July, 1810, when the government at Buenos Aires declared itself, the Banda Oriental was among those provinces which refused to join in secession. For this reason the Spanish viceroyalty was moved to Montevideo, from there the viceroy declared war, in behalf of Spain, on Buenos Aires.

But the seeds of discontent were sprouting in the Banda Oriental also. A member of the Spanish forces in the province, named José Gervasio Artigas, fled to Buenos Aires and, with the rank of Lieutenant-Colonel, was put in charge of 150 men. In his absence a general uprising had begun, in which the gauchos took a leading part. When Artigas, himself a gaucho, returned, he was met at Colonia by a large band of armed countrymen who hailed him as head of the revolutionary forces.

A succession of victories led Artigas to the siege of Montevideo. But the besieged garrison of Colonia escaped to Montevideo, and the attacking force had to be reinforced by Argentine troops under José Rondeau. In desperation, the viceroy appealed to the Queen of Portugal, sister of the Spanish king, who was in Rio de Janeiro. The reply came in the form of a swarm of Portuguese troops who crossed the northern border and threatened to overrun the country. Alarmed, the revolutionary government in Buenos Aires made a hurried treaty with the viceroy, agreeing to withdraw, and to recognize the authority of Spain throughout the Banda Oriental.

The Exodus

Artigas, bitter at the turn of events, bided by the terms of the treaty, but began to fight in his own way. He sent out a call to all patriots, to which over thirteen thousand men, women, and children responded. Under the escort of three thousand soldiers and four hundred Charrúa Indians, these people began a mass exodus from their native country. Crossing the Uruguay River at Salta, they landed in Argentina, and settled down to await the day on which they might return to their own independent country. Meanwhile, the Portuguese, finding no opposition, overran the country, sacking and pillaging. The Spanish Royalists did nothing to stop them, but General Manuel Belgrano in Buenos Aires was able, through British influence, to make a treaty with Portugal, thus robbing the royalists of their allies. Then followed a two-year siege of Montevideo.

During this period, Artigas regained the power and prestige he had lost when Argentine commanders superseded him. He convened a national congress of an independent Uruguay. This body elected him President and Military Governor. In 1814 Montevideo capitulated, and then followed a long struggle between Buenos Aires and Uruguay. The rest of the Argentine provinces allied themselves with Uruguay against Buenos Aires, but before any agreement could be reached, the country was again invaded by the Portuguese, this time with an irresistible army of 12,000 men.

With Artigas defeated and in exile, the country looked to another leader, Colonel Juan Antonio Lavalleja. Starting out with thirty-three officers and men (mostly officers), Lavalleja sallied into Uruguay. One minor victory after another added to his forces, and he finally besieged Montevideo and its garrison of 1,500, with a force of 100 patriots. By means of a colossal bluff he succeeded, arousing the citizens of Uruguay to a patriotic frenzy. Soon the whole country was in arms against the enemy.

While hostilities were still in progress, a government was formed. In August, 1827, Argentina and Brazil formally acknowledged the independence of Uruguay, and a provisional government was set up. On May 1st, 1829, the government dignitaries, in a formal ceremony, entered Montevideo, and the Republic of Uruguay was officially born.

Liberty had come, but not peace! Lavalleja, the leader in war, became a despotic dictator. When a constitution was written, and his rival, General Rivera, was elected President, Lavalleja began plotting against him. A rebellion of the Charrúa Indians that he instigated resulted only in the extirpation of that race. A rising in the capital was more successful, and the National Assembly was intimidated into making Lavalleja President in Rivera's absence. Hastily returning to the capital, Rivera, at the head of his army, chased Lavalleja into Brazil. But the tyrant de Rosas had now come to power in Argentina, and he too had designs on Uruguay to which country many of his political enemies had fled. To help Lavalleja, he despatched an armed force to capture the town of Meloa, but, Rivera's men catching up with them, they too fled to Brazil.

Thereafter the tides of battle rolled back and forth over the grasslands of the campo. The end came when the combined forces of Uruguay and Entre Rios crushed de Rosas's troops and compelled him to flee to Europe, in 1851.

This long succession of wars had left Uruguay free but desolated and impoverished, a situation that led to an almost continuous succession of rebellions and uprisings. Between 1868 and 1870 an epidemic of cholera spread throughout the country, followed by a financial crisis that ruined thousands of families. But progress was being made in the people's struggle for existence.

In 1869 the first railroad was completed, between Montevideo and Canelones. Two dictators and a series of presidents followed in rapid succession, some driven from office, some murdered. Gradually the spirit of insurrection died down, after a final short resurgence in 1911 under the

Colorado President, Jose Bâttle y Ordóñez. A visitor to Uruguay today would never guess that the smiling countryside had weltered in a blood bath of fratricidal strife for three hundred years.

The White Man's Country

Now the country is a strong democracy. Of the little over two and three-quarter millions population, eighty-nine per cent are of pure European stock, largely Spanish, perhaps thirty per cent Italian, many Portuguese and some Poles, added to which there is a colony of Swiss and some thousands of Germans. A third of these people live in Montevideo. The number of mestizos and Negroes is negligible. The climate of the country is mild, and ninety per cent of the land is usable for grazing or crops. But the Uruguayan prefers the breeding of cattle to the more arduous labor of farming. That is why seventy-five per cent of the land is used for cattle and sheep rearing, and only six per cent devoted to wheat, corn, oats, barley, and flax.

The leading citizens of Uruguay are not so fantastically rich as their Argentine brothers, nor so intent on displaying their wealth; there are more of them and not so much of the 72,000 square miles of land is tied up in large estates. Small farms are numerous, and over twenty per cent of the working class are employed in the freezing plants, factories, and mills. Because a large proportion of the population is urban, and there are no really remote areas (in proportion to its area it has more railroad mileage than any other South American country) most children receive a good education in the best schools of South

America. In this, as in numerous other social projects, Uruguay has long been far ahead of many richer countries on this Continent and in Europe.

For many years the State has operated industries in competition with private enterprise, and the results generally have been good. There is much legislation to protect the poor and ensure employment. Every adult, male or female, not only *may* vote, but *must*. They have minimum-wage laws, the eight-hour working day, collective bargaining, and old-age pensions. An extensive ocean shore line and moderate altitudes are largely responsible for one of the most agreeable climates in South America.

In this once-rich little country with the climate of Florida plus a much more enticing landscape, the people have every inducement to be happy, and every opportunity in normal times to be prosperous. Unfortunately, conditions in recent times have taken a turn for the worse. Attempts made to turn the country into a major producer of wheat, at the expense of the cattle-raising industry, have not helped. Actually, the wheat crop was quadrupled, but the fall-off in cattle production forced the closing of two large U.S. packing plants, the available cattle going to the national plant. This is but one example of the burgeoning of an intense nationalism which has reduced the country's foreign trade to a dangerously low level and forced other international companies to consider withdrawing. The increase in unemployment, and the curtailment of imports has resulted in serious labor trouble that has not helped the situation. The outlook is not good unless some national policies are reversed or amended.

Paraguay

The most tragic country of all in South America is land-locked Paraguay. Between 1865 and 1870, almost every man and boy over fifteen years of age was killed in the most disastrous war ever fought on these continents. What there is of the country today was built upon the wreckage of that conflict. The wonder is that it has survived as an independent nation at all.

Up to 1811, the history of Paraguay was the history of Argentina and the Spanish viceroyalty of which it formed a part after 1776. Here were the first settlements on the trail to Potosí, where the Guaraní Indians encountered the Spaniards and collaborated with them in producing a new race.

Early Settlement

When, in the early sixteenth century, the conquistadors found it necessary to produce their own food, the Indians were put to work growing it. Later they added livestock when the first cattle arrived from Spain. This herd consisted of seven cows and a bull, which were landed on the coast near Santa Catharina, Brazil, and driven overland to Paraguay.

In 1609 the Jesuits began to establish missions, and took control of many thousands of Indians, protecting them, in theory at least, from slavery. The fact that Asunción, the principal town in Paraguay, was a thousand miles from the Atlantic—a difficult journey by water—left it largely dependent on overland travel through areas infested by hostile Indians.

When the interest in the eastern approach to Potosí flagged and the Paraná and Paraguay Rivers lost their values as highways to the Bolivian highlands (Alto Peru), Paraguay became remote from the principal centers of activity and almost isolated. Very few, if any, Spaniards came to the country, and Paraguay's population was soon practically all Indian and mestizo.

Even in 1591 they knew what they wanted, and elected their own governor from among the native-born. This was the first time such a thing had been done in the South American colonies where the Crown was supreme. The contribution to progress of this governor, Hernando Arias de Saavedra, was the organization of an army of 600 Spaniards and mestizos (in the usual proportions!) to wipe out the troublesome Charrúa Indians. Sad to relate, it was the Indians who wiped out the Spaniards. That disaster led Saavedra to petition the Spanish Crown to send missionaries to do with peaceful methods what could not be accomplished by force. It was these clerics who, as we have seen, paved the way for the settlement of Uruguay, and pacified the Charrúas in the Northwest—temporarily, at least.

When the Jesuit missions were closed, in 1767, the half-civilized Indians they had taken under their protection were of necessity abandoned to their own resources. Since there were no centers of population to which they could go without being enslaved, as they could in Uruguay, most of these Indians fell back into barbarism, or were captured by the Brazilian slave hunters and spirited away. In some cases their farms remained to be developed by new mestizo residents of the abandoned hamlets into villages and towns. Otherwise, the influence of the Jesuits in Paraguay, in all probability had no lasting effects.

Little of importance to the present narrative occurred at this time in Paraguay that has not already been mentioned in connection with Argentina. In the eighteenth century, small progress was made in the development of trade in quebracho and maté. Not till the beginning of the nineteenth century did Paraguay assume any great importance in the affairs of the day.

Belgrano and the Paraguayans

When Argentina, in 1810, decided on a break with Spain, an army was despatched under General Manuel Belgrano to help the Paraguayans free themselves from the Spanish rule. But the people in Paraguay were in no hurry to make the break. They had first to be sure they would not be merely exchanging masters in substituting Buenos Aires for Spain. At present they were satisfied with the viceroy, and Belgrano was forced to return to Buenos Aires having, it seemed, accomplished nothing.

In the following year, however, the seed that Belgrano had planted in his conversations with the Paraguayan leaders bore unexpected fruit. In a sudden coup they expelled the viceroy, strangely enough without any bloodletting. By this stroke Paraguay was freed both from Spain and Argentina. The man responsible for this achievement was Dr. José Rodríguez de Francia, who at once proceeded to appoint himself both head of the country and head of the Church.

First borrowing from France the title of Consul, he became, in 1814, Paraguay's first dictator. Remote as it already was, Paraguay was even more isolated by this iron-willed ruler. All importation and exportation of goods, and all travel beyond the border were stopped except by special license. Domestic industries were promoted with a view to making the country self-sufficient. This continued till 1840 when Rodríguez died. After him the deluge! His death marked the end of an era of cruelty and murder, and ushered in two years of anarchy. In desperation, the feeble congress elected two men—Alonso López, and Carlos Antonio López, as Consuls of the Republic. In 1844 a new Constitution brought on a new Dictator when Carlos López was made President.

The Despicable Ruler

Opening up the country to foreign trade, this López built roads and assembled a formidable army, confidence in which led him to pick quarrels with both Argentina and Brazil. His reign of terror was cut short in 1862, and into his shoes stepped his son, Francisco Solano López, probably the most despicable character ever to assume sovereignty over a helpless nation.

Utterly lacking in ability, López had been educated in France where he acquired a gaudy mistress, Madame Lynch. He had also contracted a Napoleonic complex, and dreamed of carving an empire in the heart of South America. Five-feet-four and fat, he boasted of his Guaraní blood, and displayed many of the less admirable traits of his cannibal ancestors. His first acts on assuming the dictatorship were to erect a fabulous gold-and-cream palace for his mistress—it still stands in Asunción—and built up an army to a far greater strength than the size of the country warranted.

Having this weapon, López must use it. And so, on a

flimsy pretext, he declared war on Brazil. To invade Brazil he must needs cross the Argentine province of Corrientes, and this brought him in conflict with both Argentina and Uruguay. Even with these three powers united against him, López managed to prolong the war for five years by calling to the colors every male old enough and capable of bearing arms. The women were forced to work in the fields and in the production of arms and ammunition. Cholera raged in the army and among the civilians.

When, at last, Asunción had fallen, a final stand was made in the North. In four days of savage fighting, the Brazilians slaughtered practically every remaining Paraguayan. López came to an ignominious end, shooting himself to death as he struggled to escape through a swamp.

In the beginning, the victorious allies had declared they were fighting the government and not the people of Paraguay, and promised them freedom. But there was no money for reparations, and Brazil and Argentina between them appropriated about half of the Paraguayan territory. In return for loans, Argentina secured vast concessions that gave her a large measure of control over the ill-fated country. And so for six years Paraguay was occupied by foreign troops, and not till 1869 was a provisional government formed and all slaves declared free. The following year a constitution was adopted that, in theory, at least, outlawed dictatorships for ever after. But the damage had been done.

The lost territory took in lands between the Branco and Apa Rivers in the North, including the extensive yerba maté groves which went to Brazil. Argentina took over the Misiones district, and the area between the Pilcomayo and Bermeja Rivers. With this productive land gone, with practically no men and very few cattle, the people of Paraguay in recent years factories have been established for the extraction of tannin from the wood, and the liquid instead is shipped abroad. Tobacco, the second largest export in dollar value, is grown in an area north of Asunción.

For a long time the lack of labor and the employment of primitive methods have kept production in most lines at a low level. Less than one per cent of the good agricultural land was cultivated and no attempt was made to increase the crops of corn, manioc, and rice which are staple articles of diet in Paraguay. Another restrictive feature has been the lack of transportation facilities. Construction of hard-surfaced roads began in 1939, but progress has, until quite recently, been slow. The railroads, which until a short time ago could boast of no more than 750 miles of track, have been greatly expanded through the cooperation of Argentina and Brazil. The rivers, which are navigable by vessels up to about fifteen feet draft provided the major means of transportation in days past. They are again assuming importance with the development of international waterways to the sea.

The remoteness of the country and its lack of ready contact with the more progressive centers of the adjoining countries have contributed to the backwardness of the people. Their large percentage of Indian blood, while it endows them with fanatical courage and determination on occasion, gives rise to no urge toward social and economic advancement. These handicaps can only be overcome by increased national prosperity which will permit of greater and more general educational facilities and the employment of advanced methods of agriculture.

Under these conditions it has been virtually impossible to establish a fully democratic form of government in flimsy pretext, he declared war on Brazil. To invade Brazil he must needs cross the Argentine province of Corrientes, and this brought him in conflict with both Argentina and Uruguay. Even with these three powers united against him, López managed to prolong the war for five years by calling to the colors every male old enough and capable of bearing arms. The women were forced to work in the fields and in the production of arms and ammunition. Cholera raged in the army and among the civilians.

When, at last, Asunción had fallen, a final stand was made in the North. In four days of savage fighting, the Brazilians slaughtered practically every remaining Paraguayan. López came to an ignominious end, shooting himself to death as he struggled to escape through a swamp.

In the beginning, the victorious allies had declared they were fighting the government and not the people of Paraguay, and promised them freedom. But there was no money for reparations, and Brazil and Argentina between them appropriated about half of the Paraguayan territory. In return for loans, Argentina secured vast concessions that gave her a large measure of control over the ill-fated country. And so for six years Paraguay was occupied by foreign troops, and not till 1869 was a provisional government formed and all slaves declared free. The following year a constitution was adopted that, in theory, at least, outlawed dictatorships for ever after. But the damage had been done.

The lost territory took in lands between the Branco and Apa Rivers in the North, including the extensive yerba maté groves which went to Brazil. Argentina took over the Misiones district, and the area between the Pilcomayo and Bermeja Rivers. With this productive land gone, with practically no men and very few cattle, the people of Paraguay were in a sorry plight. On the women fell the task of performing the manual labor, a heritage they have not been able to throw off to this day.

The Chaco

Despite the new constitution, the difficulties of the government were many, and the struggle for recovery was punctuated by a series of upheavals. The last revolution ended in 1923, but in 1932, the country was again plunged into war, this time against Bolivia. Paraguay won the war, and a slice of territory in the Chaco Boreal, but lost a great many men and seriously strained the economy of the country.

Except for the Chaco area, the modern remnants of Paraguay are sandwiched between the Paraguay and Paraná Rivers, and most of the population is concentrated on the east bank of the Paraguay. After 1870, the growth of population was slow, in spite of experiments in polygamy, and not till 1920 did it compensate for the war losses. Few new settlers arrived before 1907, and from 1907 to 1927, the immigrants totalled something less than 13,000 Germans, Spaniards, and Italians. Of these only about half settled in the country permanently.

The largest mass immigration occurred a year later when 3,600 Mennonites arrived from Canada and Russia. They established themselves in the northern Chaco area by the Paraguay River, devoting their activities to agriculture, stock raising, and everything necessary for their existence as a self-contained community.

The People Today

Today, 97 per cent of the 1,601,000 population of Paraguay is mestizo or Indian, and although the official language is Spanish, most of the people are bilingual, and speak Guaraní. Educational facilities are poor, and about sixty per cent of the people can neither read nor write, though education in theory, is compulsory between the ages of seven and fourteen, and there are six normal and several agricultural schools in the country. There is also a national university at Asunción but the enrollment is usually small.

The forest Indians of the Chaco and upper Paraná country are low in the scale of civilization and contribute practically nothing to the economy of the country. Altogether, there are 157,047 square miles of forested highlands, vast plains, and a great deal of swamp land. In the central part of the country, including the Chaco, large estates are devoted to cattle raising. Agriculture is carried on principally in the area between the junction of the Paraguay with the Paraná, and consists chiefly of small farms of rarely more than ten acres which are operated by their owners. These produce corn, rice, sugar and cotton. From this region, too, come large orange crops which include tremendous quantities of orange leaves from which *petit-grain* oil is distilled. This oil is used in perfumes and brings the country over a quarter of a million dollars a year.

Along the Paraná are the wooded areas from which yerba maté is gathered. In the northwest, along the Paraguay River are the extensive forests from which the quebracho logs are taken. Formerly the logs were exported, but in recent years factories have been established for the extraction of tannin from the wood, and the liquid instead is shipped abroad. Tobacco, the second largest export in dollar value, is grown in an area north of Asunción.

For a long time the lack of labor and the employment of primitive methods have kept production in most lines at a low level. Less than one per cent of the good agricultural land was cultivated and no attempt was made to increase the crops of corn, manioc, and rice which are staple articles of diet in Paraguay. Another restrictive feature has been the lack of transportation facilities. Construction of hard-surfaced roads began in 1939, but progress has, until quite recently, been slow. The railroads, which until a short time ago could boast of no more than 750 miles of track, have been greatly expanded through the cooperation of Argentina and Brazil. The rivers, which are navigable by vessels up to about fifteen feet draft provided the major means of transportation in days past. They are again assuming importance with the development of international waterways to the sea.

The remoteness of the country and its lack of ready contact with the more progressive centers of the adjoining countries have contributed to the backwardness of the people. Their large percentage of Indian blood, while it endows them with fanatical courage and determination on occasion, gives rise to no urge toward social and economic advancement. These handicaps can only be overcome by increased national prosperity which will permit of greater and more general educational facilities and the employment of advanced methods of agriculture.

Under these conditions it has been virtually impossible to establish a fully democratic form of government in

Paraguay. Today it is an acknowledged dictatorship—albeit a benevolent one—but under that rule a great deal of progress is being made. With Brazil and Argentina helping to open up the country, foreign aid has been secured to develop oilfields and install a pipeline. Capital is also being sought to develop hydro-electric power from the tremendous falls on the upper Paraná River. In recent times cotton has become the leading export crop, and tobacco production has been greatly expanded. These however are but a small indication of what could be accomplished in Paraguay which has enormous untapped resources both for industrial and agricultural development that may in time transform it into one of the richest republics of the South.

B

CHAPTER 7

BOLIVIA: THE TIN MOUNTAINS

RICHEST IN MINERAL WEALTH OF ALL South American countries, yet probably the poorest in human material, is the Republic of Bolivia. Hemmed in by Peru, Chile, Argentina, Paraguay, and Brazil, it straddles two cordilleras of the Andes. Most of its people live on the great plateau between the mountain ranges, twelve thousand feet above the sea. The rest inhabit the eastern Andean slopes and the tropical plains at their feet.

Thousands of years ago, the Bolivian plateau was the home of the oldest and most advanced civilization that ever appeared on this continent—the ancient Tiahuanacos. This was the culture whose empire the Incas inherited, and the remains of which can be seen in stone structures and carvings that litter the high plain south and east of Lake Titicaca. Here, too, were the mines from which the Incas took much of the gold and silver that led to their extinction by the Spanish conquistadors—today the tin mines that make Bolivia important to the modern world.

Of the country's three and a quarter million people, those of Spanish or other European origins, who today form the governing class, constitute less than fifteen per cent, of which perhaps one third are Peruvian. About fifty-three per cent of the inhabitants are pure Indian of varied origins and speaking a variety of dialects, principally of Ayamará and Quechua. Those of mixed blood form the remaining thirty-two per cent. The proportions of course vary according to the region.

Highlands and Lowlands

Practically all of the whites live on the plateau, but most of the *cholos* (mestizos) live on the steep slopes of the high valleys called the Yungas, which separate the mountains from the low plains. On the other hand, cholos on the plateau furnish all the skilled labor, and some of the unskilled, to operate the shops and markets, and form the servant class. Naturally, there are different grades of cholos, depending upon the proportion of white blood (their ancestry), their degree of intelligence, prosperity, and so on, and there is usually a shortage of common labor.

The Indians predominate in the highlands and in the tropical lowlands, but again there is considerable difference between the two. In the highlands, the Indian ekes out a bare existence in a cold climate from the infertile soil which grows no trees, and fuel for cooking and heating is almost unobtainable

Fortunately for the Europeans, there are a number of valleys and gorges in the plateau which provide shelter from the winds and cold. In one of these gorges, 1,500 feet deep and two miles wide, nestles the city of La Paz, founded in 1548, which is the seat of government though

17. (*top*) La Paz, capital of Bolivia, takes shelter among the Andean peaks close to Lake Titicaca, at an altitude of over 12,000 feet.

18. (*center*) Mosaic walks line the fashionable Avenida Prado in La Paz, where tin once reigned as king.

19. (*bottom*) One of the famous reed boats on Lake Titicaca in the Bolivian highlands.

20. A famous ruin—the Gateway of the Sun, relic of Bolivia's Tiahuanaco civilization about which very little is known.

21. An Indian woman working in a cotton mill at La Paz, Bolivia. Modern equipment, such as this spinning machine, is a rarity in Bolivia.

22. (*top left*) A class in Bolivia is held outdoors while the new school is being built. There are now 2,000 schools in the country, and, once given the opportunity to learn, the youngsters are apt pupils.

23. (*center left*) An Indian female child with her baby brother at the Bolivian end of Lake Titicaca. The hat she wears is similar to that introduced by the Spaniards.

24. (*bottom left*) A Bolivian Indian of the highlands in festive costume—a descendant of the aboriginal civilization.

25. The Bolivian San José tin mines from which the Incas once took vast quantities of silver.

26. South America contains some of the most luxurious and ornate churches in the world. This church at Salvador, Bahía, Brazil, is a splendid example.

27. Cattle crossing the Amazon from the great breeding center on Marájo, the world's largest river island. For once the gauchos take to the boats.

28. (*above, left*) The jungle home of a Brazilian rubber planter in the Amazonas region—rainproof and cool.

29. (*above, right*) A rubber gatherer at work in Brazil's Amazonas, near Manoas. From these drainage cuts, the latex bleeds into the waiting receptacles.

30. The thriving city of Belo Horizonte, capital of Minas Gerais Province, Brazil. Founded on gold, it now depends for its prosperity on newly discovered and ample resources of iron ore.

31. A study in Portuguese-Indian miscegenation—a coffee picker in Brazil's Sao Paulo caught in a merry moment.

32. A unit in Brazil's vast Paraíbi-Pirai hydroelectric system, the new generating station at Santa Cecilia, Barro do Pirai.

33. One of Rio de Janeiro's fine avenues undergoing a face lifting—the President Vargas Avenue.

34. The Brazilian Gaucho of Rio Grande do Sul, Brazil's southern border.

35. The Christ statue on Corcovada overlooking Guanabara Bay, near Rio de Janeiro, Brazil.

the legal capital is Sucre. The reason that the Europeans settled on the plateau is that all of the tin, copper, lead, and bismuth mines, and the remnants of the once rich gold and silver mines are there.

The differences between the three regions—the plateau, the Yungas, and the lowlands, their contrasting climates and the divergent types of natives inhabiting them, has never made for a unified country. The Indians of the plateau, while they made good soldiers, were not physically adapted to fighting at the lower altitudes because they were not used to the dense air and the heat. Conversely, the Indians and mestizos brought to the plateau from the lowlands were not capable of sustained or arduous labor at that high altitude. Thus, from the beginning, the country was handicapped by a lack of sufficient manpower, and by by a high percentage of mortality among the forced labor. The highland people, in particular, had nothing in common with those of the lowlands, and they were not even united among themselves. The whites, the mestizos, and the separate groups of plateau Indians, formed three distinct and separate classes, and the cholos by no means constituted a connecting link.

War with Chile

If any object lesson in the futility of war was ever needed, the Republic of Bolivia would provide an excellent example. Formerly an important part of *Alto Peru,* with incredible riches in silver and gold buried in its bosom, the country had two hundred miles of coast line on the Pacific. Today the country is landlocked, and even worse off than

Paraguay because there are no river highways to the sea. The Pacific outlet, the loss of which changed the course of history for Bolivia, came about through war with Chile in 1879.

Like most of the South American countries, Bolivia had engaged in quarrels with its neighbors ever since it became a separate sovereign state. In Colonial days it was known as Upper Peru. Later it belonged to the viceroyalty of Peru, and then to the viceroyalty of La Plata. Freed from Spain by Simon Bolívar in the wars for independence, Alto Peru took the name of Bolivia in honor of the Liberator. General Sucre, the first President, who took office in 1826, was forced to abdicate in 1829 by a mestizo dictator, Santa Cruz, who had plans for reuniting Bolivia with Peru. This idea did not meet with the approval of either Chile or Argentina who wanted no large and powerful neighbor on their borders. When they intervened, Santa Cruz fled, leaving behind an unsettled country ripe for insurrection.

Disputes flared intermittently till 1879, when the country settled down to an all-out war with Chile. Chile won, after three years of desperate fighting, and Bolivia lost 30,000 miles of valuable territory including her maritime provinces, her ports, and nitrate fields. But Chile was not to enjoy her new-won territory unmolested. From 1881 to 1929, she was in constant dispute with Peru over rights to this area, with Bolivia pressing for concessions. Finally, Chile permitted Bolivia to use a railroad to the coast.

Battle for the Chaco

Meanwhile, Bolivia, desperate for a deep-water outlet to the sea, turned to the Chaco Boreal. Since time immemorial, the rights to this wild area had been contested with Paraguay. The development of the Bolivian oil industry in 1933 by the Standard Oil Company brought matters to a head. With rumors of oil in the Chaco, Paraguay seized some Bolivian outposts, and the war was on.

In the beginning it seemed as though Bolivia would have no trouble at all in squelching her ambitious neighbor. She had three times the population of Paraguay, a modern army and equipment including airplanes, and some mysterious source of finances to pay the bills. But the territory was made to order for the Paraguayans. They were used to living in such country and they were independent men fighting for the land they believed belonged to them. On the other hand, the Bolivians were mostly highland Indians, physically distressed in the low altitudes, fighting for a cause they knew nothing of and from which they could not possibly benefit.

In a desperate struggle that lasted three years, the Bolivians were pushed back to their mountains. But both sides were exhausted and a truce was called. Each had lost a large number of men, and Bolivia had lost territory as well. A commission of mediation took three years to decide on a fair settlement, and in 1938 gave Paraguay a major slice of the Chaco. This effectively shut off Bolivia from the Paraguay and Pilcomayo Rivers, though she was given the right to share one river port with Paraguay.

Always unfortunate in war, Bolivia had previously lost a large slice of her rubber-producing area to Brazil. The result of all this fighting was a much shrunken and isolated country that had lost important potential sources of revenue, and been inflicted with handicaps from which she could never fully recover.

The Ayamarás

Today, when we think of Bolivia we think of her mines, and of the vast wealth that has poured out of them since the dawn of history. Few of us think of the toil that went into the digging of those mines, or of the people whose sweat and blood and misery made them possible. Yet each of these mines was excavated by human hands, and the people who labored thus to make their masters rich profited not all. These were the Indians of the plateau—the Ayamarás—successors to the Tiahuanacos, who were first brought under subjection by the Incas and later by the Spanish invaders. The Incas taught them how to make their poor land more productive, but the Inca rule did not last long enough to raise them from the semi-barbaric state in which they found them.

The handicaps under which the Ayamarás lived were many and great. The perpetual cold, due to the high altitude, the lack of fuel in a region where no trees will grow, the inferiority of the soil, and the constant hunger and misery that resulted from those things. Their poor farms provided no more than a bare subsistence, and when many of them were driven into the silver mines of Potosí in 1545, and later to the quicksilver mines found in 1571, that existence became even more arduous. No wonder that the Indians grew apathetic and sullen. Life was only made bearable for them by the deadening effects of coca. So unprepossessing were the Ayamará women that few Spaniards could tolerate them as concubines, preferring the Quechuas who lived farther south. As a result they had few mestizo offspring.

Today these Indians live pretty much as they did in

those early times. Their houses are mere stone, sod-roofed, unfurnished shacks, dirty and verminous. Because of the scarcity of fuel, they have no fires to keep them warm, and they do as little cooking as possible. Such fuel as can be had consists, for the most part, of dried llama dung called *taquia*, woody scrub called *tola*, or a dried moss known as *lloreta*. Because of the high altitude, which ranges from 12,000 to 15,000 feet, water boils at around 185 degrees Fahrenheit, and things take much longer to cook, besides eating up the fuel.

Under the Incas, each family head had his plot of land and was responsible for making it produce its proper quota of foodstuffs. And always a proportion of that produce was stored against times of want. Today, few of them own outright any land at all. Usually they share their meager plot with several others. That land is the most valuable thing they possess, and they will sacrifice anything to preserve it. In Inca times their crops were limited to potatoes and *quinoa*, and their livestock consisted of alpacas and llamas.

The quinoa, which is still grown, is a cereal grain little larger than a mustard seed. It has many uses. Boiled, it makes a hot cereal or soup. The flour makes a hard bread that seems to keep indefinitely. With the coming of the Spaniards, barley, wheat, and oats were introduced, and sheep became the principal source of meat, wool, and skins. But this does not mean that the Indians were any better off. Their diet, in all probability, remained the same, and always too little.

Even now the average Indian is still largely dependent on the llama, which is the native beast of burden, besides a valuable source of meat, wool, bone, and leather. Some of the plateau area is held by large estates, and a few cattle are bred. But the Indians working for these owners are no more ambitious than their independent brethren. All depend upon the natural growth of *ichu* grass which forms both food and fuel. In the handling of animals as in agriculture, old-time methods are used and modern tools and equipment scorned. Education in these things is difficult among Indians who cannot read, and resent the interference of outsiders.

Whether they work in the fields or in the mines or conduct pack trains of llamas across the heights, these Ayamarás ease their discomforts and dull their senses by constantly chewing the coca leaf with a little lime to release its narcotic powers. When the occasion offers they also imbibe large quantities of alcohol made from barley, which they prefer to the less potent *chicha* (beer).

Since the days of the Conquistadors, the chief concern of the Europeans on the plateau has been the production of its mineral wealth. Agriculture, already difficult, has been neglected in that region and reliance placed upon other areas of the country for the necessary supply of foodstuffs. All that is grown on the plateau is therefore inadequate to supply the needs of either Indians or whites.

As for clothing, the Ayamará depends upon the home-grown wool of the llama, or perhaps of a sheep, which his wife weaves into cloth. Upon his head is a close-fitting cap with long pendent ear flaps; under his ragged poncho a long shirt-like garment hanging over well-worn trousers, with each leg usually split up the back. In the towns he may wear a pair of rope-soled sandals or *alpargatas,* but usually he seems to prefer going bare-footed. Often the whole ensemble will be surmounted by a basin-like heavy felt hat.

The plateau Indian's principal items of food are the potato and quinoa pone. The potatoes come in many varieties, often small and yellowish inside. They are stored dry —after freezing and soaking—and so can be kept a long time. The quinoa is made into a hard bread that the herders and porters carry with them.

The plateau covers about 40,000 square miles, and only the northern half has enough rainfall to be suitable for agriculture. The southern part is generally dry and largely desert. Ringed in by a series of 20,000-foot peaks, the plateau averages about 100 miles across, between two ranges of the Andes. The passes through the mountains by which access to the plateau is gained are 12,000 to 14,000 feet above the sea. Cold in the winter, the plateau is warm only during the daytime in summer, when the snowstorms are replaced by sandstorms.

Nothing about the plateau is conducive to a life of ease and comfort, but the Indians who have lived there for generations cannot be persuaded to leave it. After breathing the thin air of this altitude for hundreds of years, their lungs have become large, making them barrel-chested, and they are uncomfortable in the lower elevations.

These are the only Indians who can be used for heavy manual labor on the plateau. Beyond that there is little that they can contribute to the economic advancement of the country. Living in more or less isolated groups, lacking in ambition, and entirely illiterate and uneducated, their outlook is poor. Only a revolution in their way of life, and a close contact with the superior races will help them at all, and enable them to take their part eventually in the political life of the nation, and work for their own betterment.

The plateau, of course, did not constitute the whole of early Bolivia, though its area was larger than it is today. The original bounds extended from the Brazilian border, beyond the eastern cordillera of the Andes, to the Pacific coast. The coastal area was hot and dry and practically uninhabited, but the eastern slopes of the Andes and the tropical plains at their feet apparently were well populated. The Andean slopes and the valleys between them form what is now known as the Yungas region. Below this are the low plains and the jungle that extends to the Brazilian border. In both of these areas there lived in colonial times a number of scattered tribes and smaller units of Indians. These groups enjoyed various degrees of barbarity. Those on the mountain slopes were more settled than those of the jungles, and therefore more readily put to work growing food for the Spaniards, and for their less fortunate brethren of the plateau who were forced to labor in the mines. From these Indians came most of the mestizos (cholos) who live in Bolivia today, and form its nearest approach to a middle class.

Indians of the Yungas

The Yungas is a region of deep green valleys between cloud-capped mountainous ridges, ranging in altitude from 3,000 to 10,000 feet. The contrast between this and the *altiplano* is striking, and there is just as much dissimilarity between the Indians of the Yungas and those of the plateau.

In the Yungas the hills for the most part are covered with grass, shrubs or trees, and the slopes with agricultural crops. Half of the people are Indians and half cholos, all of whom speak Quechua. They are decidedly superior to the Indians of the plateau (*altiplano*). Most of the Yungas land which has been cultivated—a small proportion of the total—is owned by large estates, and the farms are operated by native superintendents. These men, however, are not much superior to the laborers they control; their methods are antiquated and their equipment crude. The work is done by permanent laborers who, with their usually extensive families, live on the estates; and by Indian squatters, or *faenas*. These so-called "free" Indians pay rent to the landowners in the form of labor during the harvest season, and sometimes in the form of animal or vegetable produce. The permanent workers, on the other hand, receive pay the year round, plus clothing, produce, and an adequate supply of alcoholic beverage—*aguardiente* or chicha. While most of the plateau Indians prefer the stronger drink, the Yungas cholos are content with the milder chicha.

The farm workers live in adobe or stone houses of one or two rooms, provided by the estates on which they work. The Indians, on the other hand, have houses of straw or adobe, some on the hilltops and others on the marginal lands of the valleys.

The valleys are deep and the slopes are steep, and the only connections between them are the narrow mule trails over the ridges. The Indians and cholos who do not live on the estates inhabit the scattered villages of the valleys. The great variations in altitude provide a variety of climates in a comparatively small area. In the lower Yungas, summer temperatures reach as high as ninety-five degrees Fahrenheit. In winter they rarely go below fifty-six degrees. At altitudes of around 5,000 feet, the temperature ranges are small, and the climate generally delightful throughout the year. The rainfall varies from ten to thirty-five inches, most of which falls between October and May, the higher altitudes, up to 8,500 feet, receiving the most.

These variations in atmospheric and soil conditions make possible a wide variety of agricultural products. The lower slopes and valley bottoms produce sugar cane, cacao, coca, corn from which the fermented drink chicha is made, and barley, a great deal of which goes into alcohol, together with a wide variety of fruits and vegetables. In the higher elevations the Indians grow potatoes, corn, barley, and quinoa; and also pasture herds of sheep, alpacas, and llamas.

Because of the isolated nature of the valleys, the attention of the farmers is principally concentrated on crops that will withstand slow transportation over long distances. For this reason, and because of the large demand among the Indian population for the drug, the principal crop is coca. This grows in the form of well-pruned bushes on the terraced slopes. The dried leaves are pressed into bales, and shipped on muleback to the market towns in the highlands.

In Inca days, the use of the coca leaf by the Indians was restricted, but the Spaniards, who were solely concerned with getting as much work out of the Indians as possible, found this drug an ally. Chewing the leaves with a little lime, or the ashes of quinoa, releases the cocaine, which deadens the senses. Use of the drug makes the Indians temporarily immune to the effects of cold, hunger, thirst, and fatigue. They can then work long hours without rest, and walk long distances with loads or in charge of llama pack trains.

All Indians from early youth use the drug, which, over the years has a degenerative effect. The harder the Indian works, the more coca he needs, and the largest consumers are the laborers in the plateau mines. Coca is as important to the Indian as tobacco to the white man, but little can be done to educate the Indians, develop their intelligence, or improve their conditions, until this practice is checked.

The next crop in importance to the coca is corn. The production is considerable but two thirds of it is used to make chicha—that dirty yellow fermented liquid that takes the place of the white man's beer. The rest is used for cattle feed and bread. A great deal of the chicha is brewed in the small towns and shipped to the plateau and other parts of the country where it is in great demand at prices that pay well for the transportation. The principal cereal is barley, which will grow where a good many other crops will not. This is transported as grain to the nearest towns, where most of it is converted into beer or alcohol. The one cereal that is used as such is wheat, which is grown in substantial quantities in scattered areas. After being harvested by hand, it is threshed by having oxen trample it, as they used to do in ancient Egypt thousands of years ago. The grain is then distributed to the many small mills in the valleys for grinding into flour.

A characteristic of all these crops is the low yield per acre, and the large amount of labor involved in its production due to primitive methods of agriculture. For this reason, in spite of the large total area devoted to wheat in the Yungas, a considerable amount has still to be imported.

In the hotter valley bottoms, cacao trees produce a fair volume of beans which the mestizo workers grind by hand into chocolate. The caked chocolate is then sewn into cowhide bags and shipped to all parts of the country. But the quality is poor and transportation costs high, so that very little of it is exported. Practically all the remaining Yungas crops—coffee, fruits and vegetables—are consumed locally, and little attention is paid to improving their quality. On the whole, then, the Indians and mestizos of the Yungas have available a large variety of foodstuffs, even though animals are comparatively scarce because of the small amount of pasture land available at the lower altitudes.

Oxen for work in the fields and for haulage, and mules for transportation, are raised in small numbers. As with Indian and cholo families almost everywhere, each household may have its own goat, chickens, guinea pigs, and perhaps even swine. Altogether, the life of the Yungas natives, isolated though they are, is a happy contrast to that of the plateau Indians, but it is an almost primitive level of existence and promises to remain that way throughout the foreseeable future.

The Lowlands

Separated from the Yungas by a succession of stony ridges, the lowlands to the east and south suffer from a combination of tropical heat and heavy rains. But even here there are wide variations in the climate and soil conditions. The inhabitants of the more remote regions are largely primitive Indians. Isolated on the border of this wilderness is the largest town of the lowland territory, Santa Cruz de la Sierra, with a population of 35,000. To the south of Santa Cruz is a series of settlements. In these towns live more than half the population of the area.

In the tropical forests of the northern plains live the

jungle Indians. Some of them have their homes on river banks where they spear fish and hunt animals with bows. Others live in clearings where they grow their primitive patches of cassava, bananas, and corn. In the isolated settlements, where the open plain permits of grazing cattle, transportation is principally by boats, canoes, and launches on the wide and shallow rivers. These also serve to connect the trails used by wandering rubber gatherers. These men live in palm-thatched huts mounted on stilts to protect them from the floods that often inundate the countryside. The Indians, however, are satisfied with simple shelters without sides.

Cassava is the staple food here as in most other primitive areas of South America, but it is generally boiled whole instead of being used in the form of flour. The clothing of the Indians consists largely of tapa cloth, made from the inner bark of trees. Some of them wear a loin cloth, others a sort of shirt and short trousers, while many go naked except for a woven straw hat! Clothing would not protect them from the myriad stinging, biting, and sucking insects, or ward off the scourges of malaria and hookworm.

Disease, too, attacks the million or so cattle that graze on the northern plains and scattered pasture lands, and many are killed by jaguars and snakes. The market for this meat is restricted principally to the rubber gatherers, and settlement Indians and cholos. Lack of transportation to the west makes it not worth while to fence in the stock and improve the breed. Beside which there would be stiff competition from the cattle ranges of the east and south.

The Chiquitos Highlands

In the Santa Cruz area are the high plains and hills, called the Chiquitos Highlands, which divide the drainage areas of the Upper Amazon and the Paraguay. Being at an average of a thousand feet altitude, this area is well drained and the climate is not so oppressive as that of the north. The heavy forest growth is absent, and travel is much easier. It is therefore only natural that this should be the chief area of population, and support a higher type of civilization. Here are the large cattle ranches, most of them managed by administrators for owners who spend their money, and even their lives, in Buenos Aires or Europe. In this respect the land might well be a part of Argentina. But it is far from being as rich an area as the Argentine pampa, for most of the cattle are usable only in the form of dried beef or hides. Transportation again is a handicap not easily overcome.

Besides the large ranches, extensive areas are controlled by Franciscan missions. These missions operate their own farms and cattle lands, at the expense of the Indians, who perform the labor with little or no return beyond the salvation of their souls. This they have done since the seventeenth century, with little change in methods and little improvement in the status of the Indians.

The rest of the Bolivian territory consists of land in the *Gran Chaco*. This area is mostly flat plain a few hundred feet above sea level, and most of it is flooded in the wet season. In the dry season it is parched and dusty, and always its only human inhabitants are the fierce, nomadic Chaco Indians. But this somewhat unpleasant stretch of real estate now promises to become the salvation of Bolivia, for there lies oil!

Formerly, tin formed seventy per cent of the country's exports in dollar value, but the nationalized tin mines became less profitable through a creeping inflation and uneconomic production. Then oil was discovered, and developed on an increasingly large scale, adding $30,000,000 a year to the national revenue. This promises to increase as a pipeline over the Andes to the port of Arica is put into operation. Another favorable development has been the acquisition of a railroad built by Argentina to tap Bolivia's Santa Cruz oilfields, thereby opening up other markets to the South and East. These developments, combined with the government's stabilization program, promise better days to come.

B R A Z I L

CHAPTER 8

BRAZIL: NEGROES, DIAMONDS AND COFFEE

FROM THE HUMAN STANDPOINT, THE United States of Brazil is one of the most interesting and important countries in the world. That it is a quarter of a million square miles bigger than the continental United States, or that it produces about sixty-five per cent of the Latin-American coffee, is of little significance beside the fact that it stands as an object lesson in racial tolerance and the possibilities of racial fusion that the world would do well to heed.

Ever since this enormous land was taken under the wing of Portugal, almost four hundred and fifty years ago, black men, brown men, and white men have lived there together in comparative harmony, intermarrying, and on a basis of racial equality, when once the status of conqueror and conquered, of master and slave, had lost its early significance. Here is played out the tremendous drama in which a nation of sixty-one million people has been built out of the fusion of divergent races, proving that color of skin, and origin, are of little account in the final reckoning.

Land Without Treasure

Such a mixture of races was inevitable in the peopling of this eastern section of the continent. In the earliest days of the Portuguese invasion, when it became evident that the country must be occupied or lost, the immediate need was for labor. Instead of the treasures that awaited the Spaniards on the other side of the Continent the Portuguese encountered only fertile lands and, usually, friendly Indians. There was little need for soldiers, and so, instead of conquistadors, the King sent aristocrats and men of wealth to develop the country's natural resources as best they saw fit. Vast areas of land were allotted to them (on the not-too-accurate maps of the day) and they were then left to their own devices.

The immediate needs of these brocaded pioneers were men to work the land, and women for their pleasure. For these things they turned to the Indians, but the Indian women were far more agreeable (and prolific) as concubines than the men were as workers. For seventy years the Portuguese struggled to live on the labor of the Indian slaves, a situation complicated by the fact that the enslaving of the aboriginals was, technically, illegal. Had not the Pope declared them to be human beings with souls? Jesuit missions throughout the interior, gathered numbers of the Indians into villages where they could be taught the catechism and be put to work. For many of the brown men this spelled sanctuary from the raids of the slave hunters. Others, who could tolerate no servitude, whether by priest or plantation owner, fled to the depths of the forests.

Slaves from Africa

Soon the slave traders—mostly half-breed Indians themselves—were raiding the missions and selling the trained Indians into slavery on the *fazendas* (plantations). But even with the growing numbers of Indian slaves, the labor situation was little improved. The Indians died in great numbers of overwork or disease, and many ran away or were killed trying to do so. It soon became evident to the *fazendeiros* (estate owners) that the only real and permanent solution would be the importation of Negroes, such as they had been used to in Portugal.

The first substantial cargoes of Negro slaves were brought into Brazil in 1574, and proved the salvation of the country. This use of Negro slaves was perfectly lawful, since the Church looked upon the black men as subhuman, with no soul worth the saving. Unlike the Indians, the black men were not affected by the tropical heat, and could undertake arduous work without ill effects. But this was not the whole reason for the success of the enterprise. Much of it lay in the character of the black men themselves who were, for the most part, far from being the woefully ignorant savages we usually presume them to have been. Even in the 16th century, some of these Negroes had reached a state of civilization in their homeland far above that of many Indian tribes inhabiting the jungles of Brazil.

Raiding the entire coast of Africa, the slave traders brought their human cargoes from the Niger, the Congo, and the Nile, from the forests, and the grassy highlands, and the plains. The blacks represented many tribes and many cultures, from Bushmen and Hottentots to the tall Nilotic Sudanese. There were Bantus and Kaffirs, who for centuries had bred huge herds of cattle on Africa's fertile plains. There were communal farmers from the Congo, keen tillers of the earth who knew the use of fertilizers and the value of irrigation.

But, far more astonishing than all of this, is the history of the Gold Coast Ashantis, the Kaffirs, and the Zulus, and their brother Africans of the Ivory Coast and the Bight of Benin. For among these people the world's iron age was born! Four thousand years ago, ancient dark-skinned men of Africa learned how to smelt iron from meteorites and iron ore. From this iron they fashioned weapons—the arrows and spear heads, the knives, the hoes and digging tools, and the cooking utensils and ornaments for their swarthy bodies.

Earlier, or later—no one knows for sure—they had become adept at casting bronze and brass. They even made wire from the soft copper, and were familiar with the working of silver and gold. By the 13th century, A.D., they were making metal objects in such quantities that traders were buying them for export to India! By the time the slave traders began shipping these black men to Brazil (and elsewhere) their metalworkers had been developing their art for 3,500 years. In that time they had also become skilfull craftsmen in many other media. They tanned hides to make leather for their warriors' shields, for body coverings and sandals. They cultivated cotton, and made embroidered rugs, often set with gold ornaments and precious stones. The weaving and dyeing of cloths, and the making of baskets in intricate designs were commonplace things to them. They carved images and charms, and made representations of animals and people in wood, ebony, ivory, and terra-cotta, and worked in stone. At an early date they even made glass.

These were the aboriginal black men who built themselves towns of twenty thousand inhabitants, and villages in which the whole people specialized in some form of manufacturing, or trade. Trading between towns was possible because the people had long learned to cooperate, both in peace and war. Many of their political units incorporated numbers of tribes and villages. More than 3,500 years ago, the black Kingdom of Ethiopia was powerful enough to conquer Egypt and rule it for a century.

The Moors and Arabs had a vital influence on the Negro civilization, giving millions of black men the Arabic language, spoken and written, and the Moslem religion. From the seventh century on, contacts between the two worlds—the white men's and the black men's—were frequent and productive for both of them. By the tenth century, a number of great Negro States were rising or flourishing—the Moslem Empire of the Songhai which lasted six centuries, the Ghana, and the Mellestine, are probably the best known. When Brazil was discovered, the Songhai Empire occupied all the central part of the western bulge of Africa, as far east as Lake Chad—over a million square miles of territory. Not long before, when Vasco da Gama skirted the east coast of Africa in his search for the Spice Islands, it was Negro pilots from the port of Malindi who steered him twenty-five hundred miles across the Indian Ocean to Calicut.

Of such stuff were the sturdy black men dragged from their homes and shipped like cattle in foul, stinking, hell-ships to slavery in the New World. Those that survived the passage were surely able to withstand anything. In the colony it soon became a common saying that the only way to kill a black man was to hang him, and that any Negro was worth four Indians.

the men died in resisting capture. Likewise their habits were repellent to the Europeans so that a sort of natural selection prevailed when it came to seeking concubines. The Portuguese, fortunately for posterity, took the more cleanly, and higher grade Indian women of the agricultural tribes. The escaped Negro slaves, in later days, may not have been so particular.

The Indian population of the Brazilian territory was scattered along its myriad rivers and its coast, and was never very large. For one thing, the Indian was nowhere so fertile as the Negro. For many of them food was scarce, and they suffered from diet deficiencies. The number of mouths to feed, fortunately, could always be controlled by the practice of abortion. With some of the tribes, if the mother died in childbirth, the baby was buried with her.

In common with a great many other primitive peoples, the mothers suckled their offspring until they were four or five years old. Polygamy was general, and usually took the form of replacing the first wife with a younger and more active one as age overtook her. Since the women did most of the active labor, a strong and energetic wife was a necessity for every Indian.

With some exceptions, the prevailing belief was that all objects were possessed of spirits or souls (animism) of either sex. A female spirit would not respond to a male Indian and a male spirit would not work for a woman. Whether or not this idea was conceived by the males for their own benefit we shall never know. But its effect was to make the spirits of all growing things feminine so that only women were likely to be successful in agriculture. To the women then fell the lot of preparing the ground and planting and tending the growing things, once the men had cleared the land. The idea was extended to the making of various objects, such as hammocks, which fell to the lot of the women.

With the coming of the Portuguese this picture was changed in many respects. The gathering of the Indians into tight communal groups and the changing conditions under which they were forced to live by the missions (including the donning of garments) gave rise to epidemics that caused many deaths. The activities of the slave raiders, resulted in the killing off of many of the males, who would not have lived long as slaves in any event. So many of these Indians were used to living in the leafy fastnesses of the forests, where the temperatures were cool and the air damp, that they could not adapt themselves to laboring in the heat of the sun. Add to this the fact that they were not accustomed to sustained heavy work, and it is easy to understand why they were so inferior to the blacks as slaves.

The rapid expansion of the sugar plantations in the middle fifteen hundreds, brought a labor crisis. The fidalgos were greedy for wealth which they needed to rule their individual empires like the feudal states they were. That wealth lay at their fingertips, if only they could get the necessary labor. The importation of Negroes had increased vastly, but still it was impossible to supply the demand at reasonable cost. Scarcity raised prices in the slave market and the fazendeiros looked once more to the Indian as the answer to their problem.

Caribocas/Mamelucos

By this time there were large numbers of *caribocas* (mixed white and Indian) roaming the coastal plateaux. Like their white sires, these half-breeds valued only two things—liberty and riches as represented by a life of ease. They were natural adventurers, intelligent and energetic. A common thirst for adventure drew them together, and the cool highlands, far above the hot coastal plain, where the Portuguese law could not reach them, drew them like a magnet. Here they founded the town of São Paulo, destined to become a great city centuries later, as a center from which to raid the vast plains and forests (the sertão) that surrounded them on every side.

Banded together in groups of a hundred or more, these *bandeirantes*, who called themselves *mamelucos*, began their mass raids on the people of their Indian mothers. They captured Indian slaves by the thousands, and sold them to the fazendeiros. This was a sure source of wealth, but there was always the lure of the unknown—the possibility of finding riches in the form of gold or other precious metals. Their expeditions often lasted months or even years. They took with them their women and food supplies, and seed for planting in case their provisions ran out. The captured Indians they set work to replenish their larders, and took such women as they fancied to share their hammocks. From their point of view, life could offer no more.

When the Jesuits established their "reductions," in which whole tribes were baptized and laid aside their blowguns for hoes, the work of the bandeirantes was made that much easier; the human "cattle" were corralled, ready for them. These expeditions took the mamelucos far afield. They ranged the entire length and breadth of present-day Brazil, and even penetrated Ecuador as far as Quito! They were, without doubt, the Indian-fighting frontiersmen of their day, and their explorations and conquests extended the boundaries of the country far beyond the original border line laid down by the Pope.

As frontiersmen, the mamelucos were occasionally invaluable in helping keep peace, and subdue any incipient uprising on the part of the Indians. But, at other times, it was the Indians themselves who were called upon to suppress their ambitious brothers. Too often their only reward for this service was slavery or death, thanks to the treachery of the white men.

In this way the Brazilians got their start as a nation; a handful of white men mixing their blood with that of Negroes and Indians to an incredible degree. Negroes mixing with Indians, and half-castes of all kinds repeating the process through centuries, and the race growing whiter as generation succeeded generation. Under such circumstances there could be no distinction based on the color of a man's skin. It was, however, a long time before the law took cognizance of the social fact.

An historical occurrence of note that introduced still another element into Brazilian pattern was the conquest of the northeastern portion of Brazil by the Dutch in the first quarter of the seventeenth century, when the King of Spain became ruler of Portugal. Spain had taken over all Portuguese territory, and Brazil was therefore fair game for Spain's enemies. The Dutch invested the whole coast from Maranhão to Sergipe, and all they came for was plunder. They had no intention of colonizing the territory, but when they departed a dozen years later they left behind them a goodly number of blue-eyed, tow-headed youngsters as their contribution to the basic stocks of the Brazilian race.

The Gold Strike

The next event of consequence in Brazil was the discovery of gold in 1693. Up to this time the landholders had confined their plantations to the coastal plain, and concentrated on making fortunes in sugar. In Pará they had turned to cacao. When news came of the discovery of gold in the State of Minas Geraes, nine tenths of the coast population joined in a mad rush to the interior, the fazendeiros taking slaves with them to do the hard work. New fields and gold-filled rivers were found in the Goyaz and Matto Grosso areas, and the once concentrated population was quickly scattered over millions of square miles of hitherto unknown land. The sugar estates *(engenhos)* shrank almost to nothing, and never did regain their former importance. Thousands of immigrants were attracted from Portugal, England and France. Herds of cattle were driven hundreds of miles overland to the new centers of population, farms were established, and hundreds of towns founded.

In 1727, the discovery of diamonds in the goldfields increased the popular excitement, but the Portuguese government stepped in and a large area was declared Crown property. Gradually, the whole plateau was explored for gold, and new discoveries in the west led to the founding of the river port of Cuyabá, and the establishment of the vast State of Matto Grosso. Since the leading gold production centers were only two hundred to three hundred miles from Rio de Janeiro, that port quickly assumed first importance in the national life. For the first time, Brazil was exporting to the mother country something besides sugar, and the way was being paved for expansion and independence, when the time should be ripe.

This discovery of gold changed the whole nature of Brazil. It brought in large numbers of white people, and scattered the population thinly over a vast area. This was no rising tide of civilization, but the spotting of isolated frontier towns that were incapable, because of distances and terrain, of co-operating for their mutual benefit. This spreading of the population so thinly was therefore far from beneficial to the country as a whole. The individual gained more freedom, but that freedom often degenerated into license because the law was less able to exercise control. The majority of the population was no longer controlled by the rich fazendeiros, and there was no effective substitute in maintaining law and order.

On the other hand, the great plateaux were for the first time developed. Forests were cut to provide lumber for the building of towns; roads were constructed, crops planted, and the cattle industry put on a firm foundation. Sugar was still produced in the north-east, tobacco in Bahia, and hides were soon being exported in large quantities from the highlands. When the gold began to run out, toward the end of the eighteenth century, thousands who had gleaned small fortunes were on their way to poverty again. The time had come for them to realze that the true wealth of the country lay in the fertility of its soil and the honest labor of its people.

Coffee was introduced into Brazil in 1727. A thousand seeds and half a dozen seedlings were planted in Pará. The famous *terra roxa* (red earth) of this region, six to nine feet deep, proved wonderfully fertile. The 3000-foot high central plateau of eastern Brazil provided the most desirable conditions with a moderate climate and dry winters for the gathering and preparing of the coffee. As a result of these favorable conditions the cultivation of coffee rapidly spread over the States of São Paulo, Minas Gerais, Rio de Janeiro, and Espirito Santo, and today there are three billion bearing trees.

Large numbers of workers drifted from Minas Gerais into São Paulo province when coffee began to constitute a major enterprise. The wealthier ones became coffee planters, and the rest found employment of various kinds. The more adventurous of the destitute miners disappeared into the sertãos of the north-west, many to form pastoral settlements where they made a precarious living from the raising of cattle, or operated subsistence farms. The important thing is that they maintained these scattered settlements, an arrangement that prevented much progress being made in raising their standards of living and education.

In addition to the settlements, a great many single houses for rural workers were scattered over the large estates. On other estates the fazendeiros gave a piece of land for the building of a church, and permitted the clergy to supervise the small community of land workers that sprang up around it. In this way large numbers of small villages were established as labor pools for the estates, thus further complicating the problems of attacking illiteracy and unhygienic, primitive ways of living.

The Royal Family Arrives

In 1807 Napoleon took the throne of Portugal and handed it to his brother Joseph. The Portuguese Royal Family were quickly on their way to Brazil aboard a British warship, arriving at Bahia, the capital, in 1808. A few

36. Santiago, the Chilean capital, lies between the towering Andes and the Pacific Ocean, well watered by the melting snows.

37. The famous statue "Christ of the Andes" in the La Cumbre pass, symbol of eternal peace between Chile and Argentina.

38. Chile's split-level city, Valparaiso, is tied together by funicular railways which climb the cliff between the lower and the upper parts of the city.

39. The snow-capped Andes Mountains tower over the wooded valley in which nestles the capital of Chile—beautiful Santiago.

40. An Araucanian Indian woman from Temuco, Chile, in festal attire, representative of an unconquered race.

41. (*above*) Modern Bogotá, capital of Colombia, with its cathedral and government buildings on the main plaza. Note the gridiron layout of the streets where once the ancient Chibcha capital stood.

42. (*right*) Picking coffee berries near Manizales, the coffee capital of Colombia. Thanks to the moderate altitude, Colombian coffee is in great demand because of its mildness. Occasional banana trees provide shade from the sun.

43. (*top, opposite page*) A jungle mansion on the Chagui River of southern Colombia is raised on stilts to avoid the flooding river. Dugout canoes are the sole means of transportation and each family needs several.

44. (*bottom, opposite page*) Colombia's main highway to the interior is still the Magdalena River with its picturesque flat-bottomed steamboats and barges. Oil lines now parallel the river to the coast, and a railroad is being built through the jungle lining its banks.

45. Colombia's mountain of salt! In this ancient salt mine at Zipaquirá a mammoth cathedral has been cut from the salt rock. Mining was begun here six hundred years ago by the aboriginals.

46. The old and the new in architecture at Medellín, Colombia, a city founded by the Spanish Jews. Its altitude is 3,500 feet less than that of Bogotá.

47. (*above*) The twin peaks of Illiniza are thought to be the remains of a single giant volcano. This range of Andean peaks is one reason why Ecuador is called the Switzerland of South America.

48. (*left*) The famous Panama hats are actually woven by villagers in Ecuador's Manabi Province on the northern Pacific Coast from the local jipi-japa reed.

49. (*below*) A mounted Colorado Indian from the town of Santo Domingo de los Colorados, Ecuador, ready for hunting with his rifle. In his plastered-down hair is a modern pocket comb.

50. (*above*) Here is Quito, between two ranges of the Andes of Ecuador, 9,400 feet above the sea and almost on the equator, giving a spring-like climate all year.

51. (*center*) The Malecon Bolivar forming the water front at Guayaquil, Ecuador. Because of the shallow Guayas River, ships must be loaded and unloaded in midstream. Down this river also come large rafts of balsa logs.

52. (*bottom*) Market day at Otovalo, Ecuador, where everything from rope-soled alpargatas to hand-made-while-you-wait cigars are sold. Most of the golden-skinned vendors are Otovalo Indians, a quiet and industrious people.

months later they moved south into Rio de Janeiro. The country thus became the seat of the Portuguese Empire, and no longer slave to a government three thousand miles away. For the first time in her history, Brazil was now able to trade with whomever she wished.

This was the beginning of Brazil's economic independence. Political independence was not achieved till 1822, when King Jaõa returned to Portugal leaving behind his son, Dom Pedro I, who at once formally declared the country free. Pedro was made Emperor, but unrest was in the air. Two provinces, tired of taxation to support an extravagant court, proclaimed themselves a republic, but were soon suppressed. When Portugal formally recognized the country's independence in 1825, she saddled it with a ten million dollar debt as a parting gift. The discontent aroused by this came to a head when a war with Argentina ended in defeat, and in 1831, Dom Pedro left for exile aboard an English ship. But there still remained his five-year-old son, Dom Pedro II, to hold the empire together.

This benevolent sovereign ruled Brazil for the next sixty-eight years. Under his benign guidance, the country prospered. Foreign engineers, scientists, and businessmen were welcomed, and public works and education became the government's active concern. The cities flourished, but large numbers of the people still lived in a state of peonage or slavery. The population now had grown to three and a half millions, of whom more than a million were Negroes, and another million mulattos. The rest were white with a large proportion having various degrees of African or Indian blood. In the forests were other uncounted red men.

In 1835 slavery was officially declared illegal, but privately the decree was ignored. During the next twenty-five years, no less than 1,350,000 more kinky-haired slaves were brought into the country, most of them to wind up in the north-east where the major part of the population was concentrated. The other densely populated center, in which great numbers of whites and half-breeds found employment was around São Paulo where the coffee industry was expanding apace.

The nineteenth century was almost half gone when the tide of European immigration began to flow. Of these new-comers about thirty-five per cent were Italians. Almost as numerous were the Portuguese, the rest ranging from Spaniards to Germans. Probably not counted in any census were the pitiful and slightly ridiculous thousand or two Southerners from the United States of North America. For ten years after 1865, these former plantation owners dribbled into Brazil, bitterly determined on the right to enslave their fellow men. Two things they did not know: that the end of slavery was already in sight in Brazil, and that no Brazilian would ever understand their intolerant attitude toward the colored people.

Slavery was finally abolished in 1888, when Princess Isabella signed the humane decree that cost the House of Bragança the throne. With the departure of royalty, and the establishment of a republic in 1889, Brazil at last entered upon its modern phase.

Droughts and Population Distribution

An astonishing feature of the development of Brazil is that throughout its history, this giant territory has remained one country. Today, Brazil occupies half the South American Continent. The rest of the area is taken up by nine

Spanish republics and three colonies. In remaining united, Brazil escaped the misfortunes that befell the Spanish countries, whose physical divisions have engendered intense nationalism, dividing the peoples and giving rise to endless quarrels and bloody wars. Today, in spite of its mixed origins, the population of Brazil is homogeneous, and there are no large national groups that are difficult to assimilate, except perhaps the quarter-million Japanese imported since 1908 at times of acute labor shortage. On the other hand, the land is still thinly populated in many areas, and its people exist at all stages of social development.

In the beginning the land was split up into vast estates, extending along the coasts of Pernambuco and Bahia. This led to concentrated settlements, without land which newcomers could take up. This condition forced the opening up of the sertão as pastoral and agricultural lands. The discoveries of gold and diamonds gave rise to a general exodus to the south and west. A few years later, another 150,000 people left the north-east for the State of Maranhão where coffee-growing was proving a success. The same thing happened early in the nineteenth century, in the neighborhood of Rio de Janeiro. Simultaneously, other population movements were taking place from the sertão to the abandoned sugar regions, where cotton plantations were established.

Other periodic migrations were forced by climatic conditions. In the north-west, for instance, every fifteen years or so there would be a drought lasting anywhere from one to four years. In 1877, one such dry period drove four hundred thousand starving people from their homes. In this mass migration to the coast, three hundred thousand of them died!

In spite of this tragedy, these perverse humans persisted in returning to their homes the moment the rains began to fall again. These droughts were largely responsible for the peopling of the Amazon basin. In those days, Brazilian Amazonia had a population of two million or so, most of whom lived near the river itself, within a thousand miles of the Atlantic Coast. While many of them were refugees from the droughts, their numbers were greatly augmented in the days of the rubber boom which petered out in 1912. Today, large numbers of these people live in semi-primitive style, getting their food from the river and the jungle, and by cultivating tiny patches of cereals and vegetables. The more active ones are able to acquire little luxuries through the gathering of rubber or brazil nuts.

A thousand miles upriver, the port of Manãos, once riotously rich from rubber, grows slowly in a more sedate fashion, by handling the commerce of the upper river. Here the sea-going steamers pick up mixed cargoes of rubber, cacao, nuts, timber, and other commodities from interior Peru, Bolivia, Colombia, and thousands of square miles of tropical Brazil, for transport to foreign ports.

All over the western part of the country are scattered settlements, large and small, unconnected by highway or rail with any progressive center. The people, for the most part, live in wattle and mud huts *(caboclos)*, with earthen floors, and walls that harbor the *barbeiro*, an insect that spreads the deadly Chagas's disease. In other areas, particularly those settled by European immigrants, tidy houses of sawn wood, or brick, often with tiled roofs, dot the landscape. Log cabins are unknown in Brazil. But in all these remote districts the problem is the same—how to establish rapid and cheap communications (or any communication at all!), spread education, and improve living conditions.

Not that the Indian-blooded natives seem to care very much. The land is still fertile, and their wants are few. Any man, aided by a sturdy wife, can put up a house, and make himself a table and a stool or two from the trees he cuts down in clearing his tiny plot. He has no social status to maintain, beyond appearing as idle as the next man. Besides, houses are made for shelter, not comfort! If he needed to buy anything he could always go into the forest and gather a few *babassú* nuts for which there would always be a market. Such apathy presents a problem for any government that recognizes the waste represented by the ignorant and unproductive!

About fifty millions of Brazil's people live in such rural areas, and only ten million or so in the towns. Rio de Janeiro, the capital, is the biggest city with a population of nearly three millions. São Paulo comes next with perhaps half a million less. Almost five per cent of the country's people are foreign-born—Spanish, Japanese, Poles, Germans, Austrians, and Syrians, to list them in order of diminishing numbers; and most of them live in urban centers.

Decline of the Sugar Estates

But the number of small farmers has grown and is still growing. Not so many years ago, the declining sugar estates were given an extra push toward oblivion by the establishment of central sugar mills. Large sugar processing companies began buying up the old plantations, and forcing out of business the patriarchal proprietors whose families had operated their *engenhos* for hundreds of years. Coming on top of the freeing of the slaves, this competition was too much for the planters who retired from the unequal contest with as good grace as they could muster.

The purpose of the mills was to assure themselves of adequate supplies of cane at reasonable prices. Quite a few of them soon found that they had more plantation area than they could handle with the available labor. They therefore split some of them up into small sections which they rented to individual farmers on a share basis, usually fifty-fifty; that is, they would take half and buy the rest.

This was but one aspect of the trend in the late nineteenth century to encourage small holdings, preferably on a cooperative basis. The government recognized that the more individuals who had a stake in the national prosperity, the stronger could the country be, and strength was vital in a land so big as this one. The logical procedure was to turn as much of the rural population as possible into landholders, or least producers. Both the government and private companies undertook to colonize favorable areas by planting settlements connected by adequate roads with their markets. The government also undertook to see that each settlement had a good and sufficient water supply, a public health center, a school building, and both teachers and an approved curriculum.

Since illiteracy averaged around 65 per cent in the rural areas, the need for education was obvious as a means of creating new standards, and markets to fill the increasing wants. To a large degree this plan was successful, wherever it was possible to apply it, in creating a moderately prosperous farm population. The children of these farmers, receiving the benefits of education, grew up to become middle-class citizens, the skilled industrial workers and business employees who left the country for the city. But all of these things cost money, and government money means taxes, but not much can be extracted from a population of poor people.

The Outlook

Today, luckily, the position has changed considerably for the better—the nation as a whole achieving an increasingly high standard of literacy. The overall percentage of literacy—48.6 per cent of the population ten years of age and over can read and write—does not of course mean very much under the circumstances of population distribution described. The major cities such as Rio, São Paulo, Pernambuco, Bahia, Porto Alegre, and many others are equal to the best anywhere in the world. They can boast not only of the finest in architecture and transportation facilities, but the highest standards of living and culture. There are eleven universities, of which seven are state supported and one owned by the federal government.

Coffee has for long been Brazil's chief export, representing some 70 per cent of the nation's export income, but this is only one of a wide range of agricultural products shipped abroad. Exports of cacao, rice, wheat, maize, tobacco, cotton, etc. have continued to increase year by year. Further expansion in foreign trade is expected with the opening of extensive manganese mines in the Matto Grosso. Industrialization however progresses slowly, waiting upon the development of the country's vast resources in coal and iron.

With a sound economy, and these tremendous reserves of natural wealth, and with a stable social-democratic government such as that ushered in by President Juscelino Kubitschek de Oliveira in 1956, the country should remain strong—and willing as well as able to aid its less fortunate neighbors as it did Paraguay in the matter of railroads not long ago.

C H I L E

CHILE:

CHAPTER 9

NITRATES AND INQUILINOS

CHILE IS A STRING-BEAN-SHAPED STRIP of land hanging on to the western shoulder of the Andes. It begins with Tierra del Fuego and stops short, 2,660 miles farther north, at Peru. But its peculiar shape is not its only claim to fame. First, it was inhabited by an unconquerable race of Indians who have left their mark upon the nation. It was possessed of enormous natural wealth that once gave it world importance. Today, it leads South America in practical attempts to improve the lot of the laboring classes. These are the things that make a study of the country particularly fascinating, for they all have had a vital influence in shaping the future of the major portion of Chile's people.

The geographical layout of the country has had a great deal to do with its expansion in several directions, and its natural resources have had no inconsiderable effect on its population distribution. Although it is over two thousand miles long, the country is, on an average, no more than 110 miles wide. Of its 286,396 square miles of territory, more than 70 per cent is mountainous and rugged, and much of the land is of no use at all.

Theorists are fond of pointing to the strange proportions of this country as influencing its development. The truth of the matter is that neither its shape nor its location at the extremity of the continent have had much effect on its trade or communications.

Doubtless if the Andes had been a little lower, its history would have been different; its climate certainly would. In all probability it would have been absorbed into Argentina, but since the Andes could not be ignored, Chile has maintained its separate identity, with little fear of hostile action on the part of its eastern neighbor.

Since the earliest times, Chile has traded across the many low passes, and with Peru, while maintaining an important flow of commerce into Spain. She has sent wheat, wine, hides, dried fruits and meats, minerals and manufactured goods to Peru. In return she has received large quantities of sugar from her neighbor, and textiles, rice, cacao, tobacco, salt and indigo from Central America.

The trade balance for a very long time was in the favor of Chile, and only in times of war did the country suffer from her isolation from Spain. In any case, it is not the topographical features of the country so much as its differences in climate with changes in latitude which are effective in influencing its economic activities. Had it suffered unduly from its relative isolation, it would hardly be today, as it has for a long time past, one of the three leading nations of the continent.

The opening of the Panama Canal undoubtedly benefited Chile, just as it did Peru and Ecuador, in lowering costs of transportation of products destined for northern countries and Europe. But a great deal of Chilean commerce still goes by way of the Straits of Magellan. Length, not location, is Chile's greatest handicap to expansion, and improved transportation can do little to offset that.

The Nature of the Country

Chile is separated into three natural divisions—the northern desert, rich in minerals; the central area which holds everything necessary for an independent and progressive civilization, including the climate; and the southern section most of which is too rugged, too heavily forested, too damp, cold and dull to prove attractive for human habitation—the one exception being the huge grazing areas of Tierra del Fuego which the country shares with Argentina.

This southern part is the largest section, a thousand miles long, with little lowlands area, much of it reaching an elevation of 10,000 feet. But here are tremendous forests providing vast untapped resources of lumber, and swift mountain streams that could supply all the electric power the country could ever need. Only at the extreme southeast, where the Andes sink into the sea, are there grassy plains that are ideal for the rearing of sheep.

Along the western coast of Chile there is a range of low mountains, and between them and the Andes is a fertile valley in central Chile, and a desert plateau in the north. The central valley and its coast is about six hundred miles long, and in this area live ninety per cent of Chile's seven million people. This is an ideal agricultural region, having a range of soils and climates to produce everything from wheat to tropical fruits. Furthermore, it is rich in mineral resources, some of which have scarcely been tapped, including the coal and iron that make it the envy of its neighboring nations. Part of this section is a large and important island called Chilóe. It lies close to the mainland, about a hundred miles south of Valdivia, and is heavily forested.

Separating Chile from Argentina is the main range of the Andes, on the crest of which stands a giant statue of Christ. Into the base of this monument is carved the legend: "Sooner shall these mountains crumble into dust than Argentines and Chileans break the peace sworn at the feet of Christ the Redeemer." Cut through the pass on which this stands is the tunnel of a trans-Andine railway, 10,452 feet above the sea.

In feeble contrast with the 20,000-foot mountains, the northern zone between Chile and Peru is a 1,000-mile desert, in the heart of which is the largest mining center of South America. In the early days this desert was a place to avoid, and the conquistadors came down from Peru into Chile by crossing the Andes from Argentina. Today, thousands of white men and Indians live there by piping water down from the melting Andean snows, or laboriously dragging it over the desert in tank cars. Under that sterile surface lie untold riches in chemicals and copper.

This, very briefly, is the physical nature of Chile, the rugged, and often indescribably lovely, background against which a young and striving democracy is unfolding. In all South American countries there is a vast gulf between the governments and their humblest citizens. Even revolutionary changes in the governments, or in the financial condition of the country, may have little or no effect on the little people who possess nothing and live so close to Mother Earth. So little do such people have in the best of times that they can scarcely have less in bad ones. Boom or depression, the existence of the peon class is barely affected. The history of Chile compresses this lesson into one overpowering example, but it also shows the good that can come out of what seems to be evil, and the benefits that may spring from disaster. This goes back to the beginnings of Chile, when the Spaniards were so persistently trying to accomplish what the Incas had for so long failed to do—conquer and subject the Araucanian Indians.

Colonial Beginnings

The defeated conquistador, Pedro de Valdivia, imbibing a draft of molten gold, had left the Spaniards in precarious occupation of some few settlements in Chile, including the capital city of Santiago. For the next 100 years, constant attacks by the Spaniards, pushed the Indians, little by little, back to the River Bio-Bio. That remained the southern frontier throughout the Colonial period, and not till 1773 was peace concluded with the Araucanians and their independence recognized. Meanwhile, the settlements had extended beyond the Araucanian territory around Temuco.

The successful resistance of the Araucanians, and their determination to die rather than be enslaved, had from the first made things difficult for the invaders. In the northern part of the country—hot and lifeless desert—but few Indians lived in irrigated oases developed for them by the Incas. Farther south there were other independent groups of aboriginals who offered as little resistance to the Spaniards as they had to the Incas. These groups had established the beginnings of an agricultural civilization which was of great value to the conquistadors in founding their settlements. But as the Spaniards moved southward, the lack of Indian labor became a serious problem. The only labor they could get was the Araucanian women they captured. Seemingly, there were quite a few of these, for the garrisons, it is said, averaged four women to each man. In Valdivia, the soldiers and civilian settlers at one time had up to thirty concubines apiece! For this reason it was only a few years before a substantial mestizo population was in process of growing up. But it was a long time before there were enough Indian or mestizo men available to do the necessary work that the women could not handle.

In the seventeenth century more and more Spaniards arrived, including a large proportion of Basques. The Basques proved to be proud and independent, and less inclined to indulge in illicit relations with the Indian females. Consequently, there are today fewer of their descendants of mixed blood. In spite of the increasing numbers of Spaniards, however, the mestizo population grew at a tremendous rate during the late seventeenth and eighteenth centuries. In 1700 the total population was estimated at 80,000. By 1800 it had soared to more than half a million, the major portion of whom were of mixed blood.

From the first, Chile was a prosperous country, if an abundance of crops and livestock is any gauge. The Spaniards had brought with them all kinds of animals, plants, and fruit trees, cereals, and vegetables. Most of these things flourished in the rich soil, and the animals multiplied at a greater rate than the humans. And so the country began to settle down into the familiar pattern, the Spaniards dividing the land among themselves and putting the Indians to work on it. The notable difference between Chile and the other conquered countries was that Chile had no rich treasure waiting to be seized, nor was there an abundance of slave labor to create such wealth. The Araucanians were highly intelligent but they were nomadic, and built no town nor gathered objects and implements of gold and silver.

After the days of Valdivia, therefore, with the exception of the sporadic battles with the Araucanians, there was no wholesale bloodshed, nor even widespread cruelty that forced Indians into the mines. The tenor of living was more leisurely, and unmarked by the fierce passions that sudden riches unleashed elsewhere. The Spaniards learned to work, and the merging of the two races was not so much marked by indifference on the part of the white men. The Araucanians were worthy of respect, even if they were heathen and heretic. There was something of a spiritual mating as well as a physical one, and the concentration of the population in this fertile valley encouraged the fusion of Indian and white into a new race that was both and neither—the Chilean. It was a happy combination in a climate that was temperate and conducive to an active life. But this did not halt the continued oppression of the peons by the landed upper class, which exists to this day in a somewhat modified form.

This was the situation when the time came to begin the struggle for independence. It was a small country and, except for the Araucanians, a united one; there were no fierce battles between loyalists and rebels, or popular uprisings. It all began with the landowners who commenced their attempt to throw off the yoke of Spain in 1810. The northern frontier at this time was slightly above the town of Copiapo, and the settled area extending south to the Bio-Bio River. Below was the Araucanian territory, duly recognized by treaty. The southern border, which was to be beyond this, was as yet undefined.

Bernardo O'Higgins

The beginnings of democracy were discernible in Chile even at this early date. The first President of Chile was the son of an Irish peddler who had risen to the office of Viceroy of Peru, Ambrosio O'Higgins. His son, Bernardo O'Higgins, was educated in Europe where he came under the influence of Francisco de Miranda, one of the great spirits of the Revolution. Back in Chile, O'Higgins became mayor of Chillán, a job insignificant in itself. But he played a useful part in maintaining peace between another Irishman, Lord Cochran, head of the Chilean fleet, and the great Liberator, José de San Martin, who did not see eye to eye on many things.

When O'Higgins became dictator, he appointed a commission to frame a constitution. In short order the property of the representatives of the Crown was seized, an army organized, a police system established. More important still, a system of free education was launched. The primary school was started by an Englishman, James Thomson, who had established a number of such schools in Buenos Aires, modeled on the Lancastrian system in England. At O'Higgins's invitation, Thomson came to Chile where he was given space for his classes in the University of Santiago. His first class consisted of two hundred pupils.

A school society was formed, with O'Higgins at its head, and a printing press procured by means of which the school books prepared by Thomson were published.

In 1822, a revolt forced O'Higgins to leave for Lima, his place being taken by another, less successful, dictator, Ramon Freire. In the next eight years a succession of Presidents followed one another without any great disorder attending their comings and goings. In 1830, a brief and small-scale civil war put Diego Portales, a businessman, at the head of the Republic. A conservative, Portales represented the aristocrats, and although there was little democracy in his rule, he maintained internal peace by his moderation. He was assassinated in 1837, but he had given the country a strong constitution, and ruled it for what he considered its best interests regardless of personalities.

But to Portales and his successors, the country consisted of the landowners and the Church. Meanwhile, however, the sons of the wealthy were going to Europe for their education, and picking up liberal ideas. At the same time, there was a growing influx of middle-class foreigners whose sympathies lay with the underdogs. Out of this ferment evolved the two political parties—the *Liberales* and the *Radicales*—to contest with the Conservatives. In 1876, the Liberales elected their first president, Aníbal Pinto. Three years later came the War of the Pacific, which not only consolidated the nation but set it on the road to true democracy.

Paralleling these events, the middle of the nineteenth century had witnessed the expansion of Chilean territory. Colonization of the area south of the Araucanian territory began in earnest, when one group of three thousand Germans, and a large number of criollos from the Central Valley took up the land. In 1864, the Indians attacked settlers who were encroaching upon their territory, and the army had to be used to subdue them. The treaty was set aside, and the territory opened up to colonization, the government selling tracts of all sizes to individuals. The result was that from 1883 on, large numbers of European immigrants were attracted to this area. About 36,000 had arrived by 1901, extending Chilean control south of the island of Chilóe.

As far back as 1843, Chile had taken possession of land bordering the Straits of Magellan, and in 1881 claimed territory in Tierra del Fuego. In 1890 these claims were recognized, and the first settlers began to arrive. In the south expansion had been, in the main, peaceful. The immigrants and settlers took over government lands in areas that had little attraction for the wealthy landowners and many drawbacks from the viewpoint of the settlers.

The Nitrate Boom

In the North, expansion took the form of an international struggle for control of the natural wealth of the Atacama desert. By 1840 the exploitation of the nitrate deposits was well under way. Chilean companies were formed to extract the sodium nitrate in territory that was claimed by Bolivia. A dispute over the boundary was settled in 1866, and the income from each mining area apportioned between the two countries. Bolivia defaulted on this arrangement, and in 1874 Chile abandoned efforts to collect the customs due. Instead, a new agreement was signed, but in 1878, Bolivia imposed an extra tax on all nitrate exports. This the Chileans refused to pay. In retaliation, Bolivia seized the Chilean properties to which Chile retorted by occupying Antofagasta, the Bolivian nitrate port. War began, and Peru joined Bolivia against Chile, but the Araucanian blood of the Chileans, plus a number of Araucanian warriors, was too much for them.

With the Bolivians driven out of the territory, the Chileans battled the Peruvians for five long years, wresting from them the rest of the nitrate "pampa," which included Tarapacá and Tacna. When peace was made in 1883, Chile retained all of this territory, and became the leading power on the Pacific coast. Bolivia no longer had an outlet to the sea.

Of even greater importance to the people of Chile than the acquisition of territory, was the fact that the war had firmly united them as a nation, and made them conscious of their powers. This was immediately evident in the first actions of the liberal President whom they elected in 1881, Domingo Santa María. Conscious of a fighting, independent nation behind him, Santa María dared to break off diplomatic relations with the Vatican, and cut down the cash tribute paid to the Church. From the point of view of the masses, other reforms were of even greater concern. The civil government took control of the registry of births, marriages, and deaths away from the priests. They gave the vote to all married men over twenty-one and single men over twenty-five, providing they could read and write. Even the Araucanians, who had done their share of fighting, were imbued with a patriotic spirit. They now considered themselves Chileans, and cooperated in the colonization of their hitherto exclusive territory. But as far as the ordinary people were concerned, the vast new wealth of the country that the nitrate fields produced was of no direct benefit at all.

For almost forty years the nitrate constituted more

than half the total exports of the country. The taxes on it often exceeded all other governmental revenues combined. The large landowners applauded this because it made it unnecessary for their land to be taxed at all. The country was rich, but the people—the laborers on the great estates, and their counterparts in the towns—were no better off. Nothing more was done for them, and their miserable "wages" remained the same. The mines themselves, largely operated by foreign concessions, gave employment to forty or fifty thousand men in boom times.

Since the nitrate was used for munitions during the first World War, production was maintained at the record level of almost three million tons a year, with a tax averaging about twelve dollars a ton. Germany, being blockaded, was forced to seek other sources of nitrogen compounds, and she succeeded beyond all expectations. The synthetic nitrates that Germany produced were cheap and plentiful, and after 1918, the United States and other countries began their manufacture also. This knocked the bottom out of the Chilean nitrate market, and wrecked the economy of the Chilean nation that had depended so largely upon it. A great number of the unemployed men from the mines descended upon the cities of the valley in search of work—or land.

The Inquilinos *and the* Rotos

And so, in the third decade of the twentieth century, the condition of the Chilean land worker was not an enviable one. In the central valley, the great landowners operated their estates as they had done in Colonial times.

The descendants of the slave Indians, mostly of mixed blood, were the *inquilinos*, working on the estates, living in miserable huts, receiving no education, and existing on a monotonous diet that a pittance of a few cents a day did not permit them to vary overmuch. Theoretically, they were free men, but that freedom was of little use when there was nowhere for them to go. The best they could hope to do was to change masters, and even that was not countenanced. Those rebels who did break away from this system became members of a large floating population of workers, the *rotos*—the "broken ones."

These rotos today are the men who work in the mines and on the railroads, on construction gangs, and on the farms in harvest time. They are the common laborers, the discontented and restless ones, having nothing but independence and making the most of that. Proud, and quick-tempered, there is nothing subservient about them, in spite of their illiteracy.

Fewer in numbers, but more important in the political scheme of things are people of the lower middle class that has developed since the late eighteenth century. Largely of foreign blood, these people include all salaried workers and the small-farm owners. Between them and the inquilinos and rotos, come the wage earners, including many women. These are the workers in mills and factories and *frigorificos* (freezing plants), separated from the lowest class by a regular income, a smattering of education, and a much higher standard of living.

At the other end of the social scale are the prosperous shopkeepers, the small business owners, the well-to-do professionals, many of them second- or third-generation immigrants, often of mixed criollo and European blood. In a still higher strata come the really rich—the owners of fifty-two percent of the land; those owning feudal-type estates averaging twenty-five hundred acres; the owners of mills, mines, banks, and other enterprises that keep them in luxury.

Finally, about thirty thousand Araucanians still live in the Temuco area, the rest having been absorbed. But these Indians, unlike those of most other countries, offer no problem to the government. They have their lands and their cattle and their horses, and constitute a dignified and intelligent, and by no means poor, section of the population. All these, and their families, then, make up the population of Chile, which today totals nearly seven millions. In the nineteen twenties there were possibly two to three millions less.

Alessandri and Modern Chile

The imminent collapse of the nitrate market brought to a head the growing contest between the middle classes and the aristocrats. A man of the people was elected President in the face of strong opposition from the upper classes. This was Arturo Alessandri, son of an Italian immigrant. He came to power in one of the most difficult times that Chile had ever experienced. With an empty treasury, and without the co-operation of the nation's most powerful group, the landholders, he could do little that he wanted to do. He fought for price regulations on food, and higher wages for the poor, as well as an income tax on the wealthy. In 1924 he was forced to resign, but was recalled a year later. His first act was to draft a new Constitution. This Constitution of 1925 emphasized the liberty of the individual and the freedom of the press. The State was divorced from the Church, and elections controlled by a non-political body. There still seemed nothing he could do about the country's basic problem, the distribution of land among the people. The Constitution launched, Alessandri retired and chaos descended on the country.

Until late in 1932, when Alessandri was re-elected, four presidents and a series of upsets left the people worse off than ever. This time Alessandri exercised a firm control under the new Constitution. He dissolved the giant nitrate combine that had been taken over by United States concerns, and formed a sales corporation with the government represented on the board. One function of this concern was to promote the use of fertilizers on Chilean farms, thereby increasing the productivity of the soil. Alessandri also instigated the formation of a Chilean oil company to compete with foreign concessions, and reorganized the foreign-controlled electric power company so that the government secured a good share of the profits.

Though he did nothing specifically for the working people of the country, he stabilized conditions, improved the national economy, simplifying the problems of his successor, President Pedro Aguirre Cerda, elected in 1938. Here, also, was a man who had begun life in humble poverty. He attained fame and position as an educator, a man whom the people could understand and believe in. Three months after his election, the greatest tragedy in her history descended upon Chile. A destructive earthquake rent the central valley, razing its cities and killing thousands. This catastrophe, striking the heart of the country, wrecked industries and played havoc in the agricultural region. The loss of crops and other foodstuffs brought quick famine.

Millions soon faced starvation, and aid had to be rushed to them from other countries.

Seeds of Progress

Out of this tragedy came the government-sponsored Chilean Development Corporation, which became the chief instrument in the work of reconstruction. In the eyes of President Aguirre here was a heaven-sent chance to improve the lot of a great part of the people. Old social laws were resurrected and new ones written; resettlement was planned, and new, modern houses put up for the workers; roads were laid out, hospitals and schools built. Systems of medical care and social security were developed, and the supply of foodstuffs at low cost arranged for these people. Milk, for the first time in Chile's history, was cheaper than wine.

Out of all this came long-range plans for the improvement of educational facilities, and for the development of natural resources as a means of establishing industries. The free and compulsory education plan apparently was a huge success for today Chile ranks third among the South American nations in having only 24 per cent of its population classed as illiterate.

Another purpose of the development scheme was to furnish jobs and provide continuous employment for the floating population of itinerant workers, and all who preferred urban life to the low-level existence offered by the large estates. Such plans naturally were opposed by the large landholders who wanted an ample supply of cheap labor on the farms. They opposed education of the laborers which might make them dissatisfied with their conditions, as would intimate contact between the inquilinos and the people of the towns.

As a result of this attitude and the resultant lack of financial cooperation, the government was forced to turn largely to foreign capital to finance its industries. Meanwhile many of the European immigrants brought with them enough capital to start small manufacturing plants. Today the situation is pretty much the same, though the government has bought up some of the large estates and set aside other lands for sale to small-holders. It helps these farmers with credit agencies and marketing facilities, including the producers' cooperatives. Other cooperative organizations are devoted to acquiring land for distribution among their members.

It is in the industrial field, however, that Chile has made tremendous strides since World War II. Oil and gas fields have been exploited in Tierra del Fuego and a refinery built, along with several hundred miles of gas and fuel lines. A thriving steel plant operates at Huachipato for which expansion is planned so that it will turn out 450,000 tons of steel ingots annually. From the beginning it has made possible many new industries and the expansion of existing facilities. Both the necessary iron and coal are mined locally. Copper, however, continues to be the major export. In 1957 the State's export revenues from copper totalled $150,000,000, from iron ore $30,000,000, and $30,000,000 from nitrates, all of which helped them weather the economic crisis that enveloped most South American countries at that time. With the stable government that has become a habit with Chileans, this temporary setback may well be the stepping stone to great advances tomorrow.

COLOMBIA

CHAPTER 10

COLOMBIA: AND THE ROCKY FINGERS OF NEW GRANADA

WHERE THE ANDES MEET THE CARIBbean Sea they split up into three distinct ranges, or cordilleras, that play hob with Colombia's economy. One of these rocky fingers straggles in the direction of central Venezuela, the middle one peters out on the Goajira Peninsula, and the third dips into the Gulf of Darien. Across these highlands sprawls the Colombian Republic, stretching its half million square miles from Brazil to the Pacific and the Caribbean to Ecuador and Peru. This rugged topography effectively divides the country into three general areas that differ greatly in characteristics and climate. Each area attracts its own type of population, and the high mountains have long imposed almost insuperable handicaps on transportation and communication, sadly hampering commercial and industrial development. Nevertheless, Colombia, by sheer dint of perseverance on the part of its white population, has, in spite of intermittent revolts and political unrest (ending in 1957 with the establishment of a bi-partisan government) led its neighbors in culture and enlightened government. Ten per cent of its national budget is set aside for education and, in addition to the national university founded at Bogotá in 1572, there are twenty-one other universities. Primary education is compulsory. Colombia's capital city, Bogotá, even today is known as the "Athens of South America," and its language is more purely Castilian than anywhere else on the Continent.

But Bogotá is not Colombia, nor does its populace represent a cross-section of the country which has an overall literacy percentage of 65 or so. For reasons which will presently become apparent, Bogotá, and in a lesser degree some of the other leading cities, have an unusually large proportion of pure-blooded Spaniards, and others of the upper class with but a trace of Indian blood. Of the country's thirteen million inhabitants, these whites constitute twenty per cent, and most of them live in the highlands where the climate varies from sub-tropical to temperate.

Like so many of its neighbors, Colombia has large numbers of brown-skinned sons. These mestizos total sixty-eight per cent of the population, and range in social rank from peons to high government officials. Indians of pure blood, descended from nearly four hundred tribes, make up only seven per cent of the people and most of them live in the tropical forests. That there should be so few of them is logical when the treatment they received from the Conquistadors is considered. The remaining five per cent are Negroes.

The Chibcha Strain

In an earlier chapter, it was mentioned that Colombia, from Bogotá to Panama, was originally inhabited by the

53. The Machu Picchu ruins of Peru, once a fabulous mountaintop Inca city in the Urubamba Valley near Cuzco.

54. Indians sell ceremonial masks at Sacsahuaman, Peru. Behind them stands one of the fantastic stone walls of the ancient Incas, each stone fitted perfectly to its neighbors without benefit of mortar.

55. (*left*) Mountain Indians of Peru, decendants of an Incan subject tribe, in their historic costume.

56. (*right*) A superb example of Spanish colonial architecture—the courtyard of the Torre Tagle Palace at Lima, Peru.

57. (*left*) On the Plaza de Armas in Lima, Peru, stands this imposing cathedral with the archbishop's palace. The latter shares honors with the Torre Tagle Palace as Lima's two most beautiful buildings.

58. (*right*) The Torre Tagle Palace at Lima, Peru, dates back to Spanish colonial days.

59. Mount Chachani's snow-covered peaks serve as an imposing backdrop for the magnificent cathedral of Arequipa, Peru.

60. The town of Pisac, Peru, lies below its terraced fields which must normally be irrigated by hand. The plowing, sowing and reaping are also done by hand.

61. A typical villager of Pisac, Peru.

62. Two native women of Huancayo, Peru, prepare vegetables for the market.

63. No race, no breed has a monopoly on beauty as these Venezuelan school children of mixed parentage show.

64. Oil and cattle are the products of Venezuela's plains, and one interferes little with the other, as this view indicates.

65. Downtown Caracas, Venezuela's capital city, is modern in every sense, thanks to the nation's wealth of oil.

66. Venezuela—"Little Venice"—gets its name from the houses on stilts first seen by the Spaniards in Lake Maracaibo. Here is a modern version of these houses at San Lorenzo.

Chibcha Indians. Their annihilation commenced with the expeditions of Quesada, Federmann, and Belalcázar to Bogotá in search of El Dorado. It was Gonzalo Jiménez de Quesada who founded the city of Santa Fé de Bogotá in 1538, after slaughtering the rulers and their families and decimating the Chibcha race. El Dorado proved to be an Indian hoax, but Quesada found the rich emerald mines, a great salt mine, and an advanced civilization that produced wonderful woven cloths, and planted vast areas of the great *sabana* (high plain) with maize and potatoes.

Here on the wide plain, 8,600 feet above the sea, and sheltered by higher peaks, was an ideal place for the development of a European culture based on the labor of Indian serfs. These Indians had reached a cultural level almost comparable with that of the Incas, but along different lines. There was more equality among them, and no distinct ruling class to dole out the lands and other favors. And there was no army. Here was a settled agricultural people, the remnants of which they found it easy to absorb. Indeed the Spaniards had more effect on the Indians than the Indians had on them. This was far from being the case in other parts of the country. To the east of the Eastern Cordillera were vast plains (llanos) that stretched to Venezuela and Brazil, with nothing to attract the Conquistadors except vague rumors of the elusive El Dorado.

In the valleys between the Cordilleras, down which flowed the future highways to the sea—the rivers Magdalena and Cauca—lived other Indians. Many of these were less amenable to civilization than the Chibchas, and tales are told of cannibals, and of white men's skins inflated like balloons. While the Chibchas had interesting, and mildly shocking, customs such as *jus prima nocte* (first-night privileges) of the caciques and priests, the valley tribes indulged in more savage rites involving wild intoxication and sex orgies. But some of these Indians too had their more esthetic moments. They panned gold and made exquisite cast and repoussé ornaments and figurines of it. It was these riches that attracted the conquistadors, and led to the settlement of the inter-mountain areas.

Gold and Oro Blanco

Far more gold, however, was found in the rivers to the west, but this was no place for white men to live. Tropical jungles and drenching rains bred miasmatic fevers and the insects that spread them. This was a place best avoided till black-skinned men and women could be brought in to work waist-deep in the chilly mountain streams. But that was to come considerably later.

Apart from Bogotá, the country, which at this period included Panama, was important only for its ports. First was Santa Marta, founded in 1525 by Caribbean pirates as a base from which to hunt Indian slaves. Shortly afterwards, the Spanish Crown sent families of settlers to colonize the place, and a priest to stop the outlaws from preying on the Indians. Then came Cartagena, with its excellent natural harbor for the Spanish plate fleet. From 1533 on, this was the headquarters for expeditions into Venezuela and Colombia. It was in New Granada (Colombia), along the Magdalena and Cauca Rivers, that Pedro de Heredia seized even more gold than Pizarro took from the Incas!

Between 1535 and 1539, Sebastian de Belalcázar, beaten to Bogotá by Jiménez de Quesada, compromised by founding the fortress towns of Popayán, Pasto, and Cali, and explored the lovely Cauca Valley in South and Central Colombia. Here the Spaniards introduced European cereals and fruits, and livestock, and large estates planted in corn, barley, and wheat. Farther west was the Chocó, whose rivers were rich in minerals. By the use of black slave labor, the production of gold was built up to a fantastic figure. At the same time an even greater treasure was thrown away—dumped into gulleys as a nuisance. This was the mysterious *oro blanco*, or white metal, that was panned along with the gold. Separated from the gold, it was thrown into holes on the river banks, and accumulated there for hundreds of years. In modern times, some of these sink-hole caches were discovered by prospectors who were aware that this despised white metal was nothing less than platinum!

The Indians, forced to work in the mines of Antioquia, rebelled so often that they were practically annihilated, and had to be replaced by Negroes. The blacks, it turned out, were far more fitted for life in this pestilential area, and able to resist the diseases that wiped out Indians and whites alike. The importation of black slaves therefore continued for many years, and many of them cohabited with Indians. From these are descended that seven per cent of the population that lives in the tropical zones of the country, principally along the shores of the Caribbean and Pacific, and along the banks of the rivers. Practically none of them reached the interior, or climbed the plateau to Bogotá.

With the emeralds from the mountains and the gold from the lowlands, it soon became evident that Colombia was a country of vast natural wealth. In addition to the key towns, others were established along the routes that had to be traversed from the coast to the interior. The only highways to this rugged country were the rivers, and the mountaintop settlements were practically isolated. To get to Bogotá meant months of travel up the Magdalena, and long marches over the mountain to the sabana.

As the colonizing program superseded the conquest and the treasure raids, more and more settlers arrived from Spain. Large numbers of them preferred the climate of the highlands. And as the population grew, the power of the Church expanded with it. The influence of the clergy in the government, combined with the oppressive and restrictive measures applied by Spain, and the remoteness of Bogotá from the ports and other means of direct contact, led to serious strife.

Throughout the seventeenth and eighteenth centuries, New Granada built up a sizable trade in wheat, sugar, hides, and cacao, as well as precious metals and emeralds, but increasing taxes reduced the flow of wealth. Internally, there was dissatisfaction, due to the difficulties of governing the country from inaccessible Bogotá, and jealousies between the widespread and isolated population centers. Unity was achieved temporarily in the struggle for independence which the great Liberator, Simon Bolívar, helped launch in 1810. But it was nine years before final victory in the field destroyed the hold of Spain, and left them free to quarrel among themselves once again. Not until 1825 was the independence of Colombia recognized by the Spanish Crown.

In fighting his final battles, Bolívar employed some six thousand English, Irish, and European soldiers released by the end of the Napoleonic wars. Turned loose in Colombia with their pay and large bonuses, many of them settled in the country that they had helped to free.

The United States of Colombia

In 1819, the Republic of Colombia was proclaimed, and shortly thereafter Venezuela was added to it, forming the United States of Colombia, with Bolívar as President and military dictator. In 1822 the provinces of Ecuador joined them to form Greater Colombia, only to drop out again in 1831.

With the achievement of full independence, the old internal jealousies again flared up in Colombia; political disorders and religious conflicts raged for almost a century. In spite of recurring revolutions involving great loss of life, the population increased rapidly. Between 1770 and 1875 it had risen from 800,000 to three millions, accompanied by a large expansion in both mining and agriculture. Toward the end of the nineteenth century, the country was exporting hides, tobacco, cinchona (quinine bark), gold, platinum, bananas, cotton, indigo, and some coffee.

Much of the coffee was grown on the mountain sides at altitudes varying between 3,300 and 6,000 feet. This coffee was quickly found to be much milder than the coffees from countries where it was grown in warmer climates, and the demand for it mounted rapidly, particularly in Europe. The immediate result of this was the establishment of large coffee haciendas on the cooler mountain slopes, and the migration of a substantial section of the population from the highlands. This activity opened up large areas of the country that had heretofore been isolated, and trails were cut to the rivers. The towns of Medellín, Manizales, and Cali grew in importance, but not till 1904, when the country was finally stabilized, was it possible to attempt modernization of transport, a factor on which the success or failure of the coffee industry hung.

Disagreement and lack of cooperation was a natural result of the distances between the centers of population, the difficulties of communication, and their differences in outlook and aims. For a long time it looked as though the country would be divided among half a dozen city-states. Bogotá was the leading city in the temperate zone, perched on top of its mountain. Its people were wealthy Spaniards, and a great many intellectuals with high, and often impractical, ideals.

Medellín, whose altitude is 3,500 feet less than that of Bogotá, was founded by a large group of Spanish Jews. These people and their descendants were enterprising by nature, and energetic. They were more given to trading than to reciting poetry, and Bogotá seemed a long way off, and not likely to offer any competition in business or industry. The growing coffee trade built up the city of Manizales, but Cali, a center both of commerce and culture dated back to 1536. This was, and is, the chief commercial town of western Colombia, and it, too, has little in common with Bogotá. Because of the difficulties of river transportation to the Caribbean, Cali's natural outlet is to the Pacific coast through the port of Buenaventura.

Among the other early and important cities that considered themselves independent of the rest of the country were Santa Marta and Cartagena. And in the river-mouth port of Barranquilla, which dates from 1620, Cartagena had a deadly rival for the interior commerce.

These were some of the factors that led the country into a series of revolutions that culminated in the great civil war of 1899-1902, in which over 100,000 men were killed. This fratricidal struggle shocked the nation, and revealed with tragic finality the futility of war as a means of settling domestic problems.

The major parties in this bloody struggle had been the Liberals and the Conservatives, and both were strong because both represented large landowners. The major difference between them was that the Conservatives were backed by the Roman Catholic Church, while the Liberals sought to abolish the Church's influence in politics, and in the schools. Conservatives held the reins in a none-too-sure grasp from 1902 to 1930. The establishment of peace in 1902 was threatened again in 1903, when the Province of Panama, through the machinations of the President of the United States, seceded and declared itself an independent state.

Under the Presidency of General Reyes, Colombia began to forge ahead and make up for lost time. With confidence in the government established, foreign capital became available for the construction of railroads and other public projects. One of the first of these projects to be undertaken was an attack on the almost insuperable difficulty of establishing rapid and reliable transportation between the centers of population and the ports. Without this, no worthwhile economic development could ever be achieved.

Journey up the Magdalena

To reach Bogotá from the Caribbean, for instance, freight had to be carried on flat-bottomed, stern-paddle steamers six hundred miles up the Magdalena. At this point it would have to be transported by wagon around the rapids, a journey of fifty miles or so, then loaded on another steamer to take it forty miles more to the terminal port. From this point on it would go by wagon another sixty-five miles up the mountain to the sabana.

A hundred miles upstream, the river becomes comparatively shallow, and littered with tree trunks and shifting sandbanks. Few of the boats, even today, ever make the complete trip without running afoul of either of these, and losing anywhere from an hour to several days as a consequence. In the early days the trip to the rapids, normally, would take ten to fourteen days, with frequent stops for firewood, and usually spending the night against the bank, warped to a jungle tree. The complete journey to Bogotá, then, would consume anywhere from a month to six weeks. Occasionally it would take three months.

Under the best of circumstances, then, the freight costs in many instances exceeded the value of the merchandise. When import duties, which the government needed badly, were added, the value of the goods became prohibitive. In the case of exports, the time lapse and the uncertainty as to when the stuff would arrive at the port made it impossible to maintain schedules with ocean steamers, and warehouse charges ballooned the costs. Under such circumstances the trade of the country was strangled before it was born.

The first of the railway projects undertaken by the

Reyes administration was the connection of Bogotá with the River Magdelena by rail eliminating the need for transshipment around the rapids. Later, a line was run from Medellín to the river, and Cali connected with the Pacific Coast. Even after this, the Magdalena still constituted a brake on the wheel of progress, as it does to this day, the new railroad paralleling the river being far from completed. But better steamers have helped, and the use of oil fuel has speeded up river travel somewhat, but there is still uncertainty and delay, especially during dry spells when the boats pile up on the sandbanks and wait there till it rains.

Some considerable relief was afforded when Bogotá was connected by rail with the town of Ibagué on the eastern flank of the central cordillera. Freight could then be shipped by motor truck over the mountains to Arménia, and put on another train for the Pacific port of Buenaventura. Despite the handicap of a break in the line, this often proves a quicker route to the Atlantic than going down the Magdalena.

It has been necessary to go to some lengths into the transportation problem of Colombia, because that is the one big factor that has not only retarded the country's progress but has in no small degree affected the condition and distribution of its people. Only when such a country is closely knit by its means of transportation and its highways can its people receive the full benefits from a centralized government, and profit by the availability of necessities at low cost.

In some respects communications are almost as important. Mail, telephones and telegraph, are necessities in any well-coordinated civilization, and they have not been secured without difficulty in Colombia. Large stretches of jungle separate the lowland towns, and wooden telegraph poles are quickly consumed by insects or rot. Iron poles are rapidly overgrown with creepers which short-circuit the lines; and so on. Interruptions are frequent, inspection is difficult, and repairs costly. Cheap long-distance service is therefore difficult to provide. Radio communication seems to be the only logical solution.

Jungle Oil

Another factor that was of great importance both to the government and the humble citizen was the discovery of oil. Sometime in 1921, an engineer hunting in the jungles of the Magdalena Valley came across oil and asphalt seepages in the neighborhood of Barranca Bermeja, three hundred miles up the Magdalena. Here again, transportation was the stumbling-block. The seeming impasse was finally overcome by running a pipe line from the wells to Cartagena Bay, a distance of 350 miles. When, in 1930, the production had exceeded twenty-two million barrels a year, the cost of the line and its frequent pumping stations was proved justified. Later, a refinery was built at Barranca Bermeja, and distribution centers established along the river to supply the steamers, railways, and industrial plants. Gasoline was then transported by steamer for delivery to river ports.

The interesting feature of this development from our immediate viewpoint, is that the oilfield in the jungle not only employed several thousands of native workers, but established a modern town complete with church, hospital, school, movie theater, recreation hall, and company store.

The houses of the workers were cool, sanitary, and comfortably furnished, and in every way far better than anything the people had ever known before. The men were well paid, dressed neatly, and enjoyed frequent holidays. From this operation the Government not only assured an adequate supply of gasoline and fuel oil for their own country, but profited from taxes on this second-largest of export items, coffee being the first.

The Brightening Skies

Additional petroleum operations are being developed in other parts of the country, and will eventually employ thousands more of the mestizo population, raising their standard of living. Already petroleum represents better than thirteen per cent of the country's exports.

A long-established industry which employs large numbers of mestizo, Negro, and zambo (Indian and black) men is banana growing. In the Santa Marta district, private growers occupy many thousands of acres, and the United Fruit Company has several times as much planted in bananas. These operations provide employment for around twenty thousand laborers who receive good wages and enjoy excellent living conditions.

Then there are Colombia's 150,000 coffee plantations and fincas (small ones) which support an aggregate of well over half a billion coffee trees. Only a few hundred plantations have more than 100,000 trees, and most have less than five thousand. The coffee-growing business, therefore, provides a living for about three quarters of a million owners and their families. In addition, many thousand of itinerant workers are employed in harvesting, of which a large number are females. Most plantations have a secondary crop, so that there are two harvests a year. In most areas there is a chronic shortage of labor for coffee picking. Fortunately, harvests are gathered at different times of the year in the various growing regions, otherwise the labor situation would be much worse.

In addition to the plantation work, there are large numbers of people employed in the coffee sorting, bagging, and transport businesses, to handle the total annual crop of well over seven million 132-pound bags of beans, nine tenths of which is shipped abroad.

Although so many people are employed in the major commercial activities, still more are occupied in farming and grazing. In the highland region, where most of the people live, the mestizos are of a high type, and the Indians more energetic than those of the lowlands, and both have a high percentage of literacy. In the low-lying areas, the primitive Indians are scattered throughout the forests, but the Negroes and zambos are found all along the Caribbean and Pacific coasts, in all hot sections, and along the river banks far inland. Those not engaged as laborers in the ports and tropical towns, have their palm-thatched huts with a small plot of land salvaged from the jungle, on which they grow subsistence crops of maize, potatoes, bananas, cassava, and perhaps keep a goat or a pig. Their diet is varied by the excellent fish they get from the river that flows past their door, and by the coconuts that usually are not far to seek.

Altogether, the lower classes of Colombia have little to complain of though there are difficulties in providing the scattered population in outlying districts with any sort of education.

Since modern, peaceful Colombia is really only fifty years old, and the handicaps of communication and transportation are so large, the progress that has been made is little short of remarkable. The airplane has helped, and the new railroads will do more to overcome the natural handicaps of terrain and distance which have to be still further conquered before the country can fully realize its great potentialities.

In recent times Colombian economic progress has been halted by political strife, but that phase has now come to an end. In 1948 the four-year dictatorship of Lieutenant-General Gustavo Rojas Pinilla left the country facing mounting inflation, and drastic measures were necessary to stop it. Since factional differences between the Liberals and Conservatives had resulted in riots that unsettled the country, the military junta which took over in 1957 from the deposed dictator formed a coalition government of both major parties. Land reforms were enacted to increase domestic crops of items normally imported in large quantities such as cotton, cacao, malt, and copra. In the rich Cauca Valley, which has known coal reserves of several hundred million tons, a coal washing plant was installed, enabling an export business in that commodity to be launched. In this area, too, extensive irrigation projects will add some two million acres of arable land.

By such determined and farsighted means, Colombia promises quickly to attain the heights of prosperity that its natural resources and its exceptional human potential should be capable of providing.

E C U A D O R

CHAPTER 11

ECUADOR: THE LAND OF CINNAMON

IT IS EASY TO BECOME LYRICAL ABOUT Ecuador, the Land of Cinnamon that lured Gonzalo Pizarro into its deadly jungles. Extravagant nature has lavished upon it the breath-taking beauty of snow-crowned volcanoes rising out of green jungles, and verdant plateaux rimmed with 20,000-foot mountain peaks. And into this setting it has placed gay and colorful Indians who pursue their placid ways in the springlike climate of the high Andean plains.

Ecuador is a poor country, with an export trade of little importance. Its area, since Peru has lopped off another slice of its shrinking Amazon territory, is estimated at 105,750 square miles, and its people number a little over three and three-quarter millions. Probably 39 per cent of them are Indians, forty-one per cent mestizos of various origins and five per cent Negroes. The pure Spanish, with a leavening of Europeans—including quite a few Germans, and the remnants of Czechoslovak and Jewish colonies—make up the balance.

Not all of the Indians are either colorful or pleasing. But all of them are interesting, either because of their background or their accomplishments, or customs and cultural achievements. Some of them live in the coastal lowlands, some in the mountain valleys, and still others lead a barbaric existence in the eastern jungles of the Oriente. They are all descendants of the tribes that the Incas found when they expanded their empire to include the ancient city of *Quitú*. Some of them were absorbed, but a great many more plunged deeper into the forests, or moved farther north where they were more safe from molestation.

Here, in Ecuador, as elsewhere on the Continent, topography and climate have had a great deal to do with the characteristics of these aborigines and their way of life. Sandwiched between Peru and Colombia, Ecuador has a great deal more coast per square mile of territory than most other South American countries. And Nature has been kind to it in many ways. The famous Humboldt current, which follows the coast of Peru, suddenly sweeps out into the Pacific as it passes the southern border of Ecuador. Instead of spilling the rains into the Pacific Ocean as it does farther south, the current graciously permits it to fall on the coastal strip, so that instead of being dry desert, the coast is clothed in tropical green. This coastal strip is about 425 miles long, and averages about sixty-two miles wide to the foothills of the Andes. It is one of the most fertile spots of the whole continent, and for long one of the least developed because of the heat and the swamps.

The Avenue of Volcanoes

The Andean range here consists of two parallel cordilleras, connected at intervals by transverse ridges like the rungs of a ladder. These ridges enclose a series of valleys, ranging from 9,000 to 13,000 feet above the sea. Towering above them are the high snow-thatched peaks of the Andes, topped by Chimborazo's 20,500 feet! No less than sixteen of these peaks are active or quiescent volcanoes. One of the most thrilling sights in the world is this avenue of snow-bejewelled volcanoes between the northern border and the capital city of Quito. The twin rows of craters with their plumes of smoke and steam, their ice-encrusted sides gleaming in the sun, their feet resting in wide green valleys dotted with blue lakes, are something that must be seen to be believed.

All through this high country are smiling mountain-ringed, tree-bordered lakes, reflecting the blue sky. Loveliest of these pools are San Pablo and Yaguarcocha—the Lake of Blood. This latter gets its name from the massacre of 20,000 Caranque Indians, by the Inca Huayna Capac, that stained its waters red. Beyond the eastern cordillera, the steep slopes of the Andes melt away toward the Amazon, their sides smothered in jungle growth. There, in the Oriente, are a few small settlements, but most of the area is given over to Indian tribes, some of whom took to the woods when the Incas came. Later they fought off all attempts of the Spaniards to enslave them and the priests to force upon them the blessings of the white man's customs and beliefs.

The Head-Shrinkers

These jungle Indians consist of scattered and unrelated groups such as the Canelos, Zaparos, and the Jívaros who hunt with blowpipes and poisoned darts. The Jívaros are probably the best known because of their quaint custom of shrinking human heads. This strange habit, however, is no indication that the Jívaros are low-grade primitives such as the murderous Motilones of Colombia. On the contrary, they are an intelligent and likeable people with less of an instinct for killing than many a "civilized" American. Some years ago, the noted explorer, Commander G. M. Dyott, lived among them for a year or more, and found them friendly and considerate hosts. Later, he returned and made a motion picture of part of the head-shrinking process. They, and most of their jungle brethren, are, admittedly, quite uninterested in what goes on outside their leafy domain. They can hardly be criticized for that. The important point, of course, is that these Indians contribute little or nothing to the country's economy, but as (and if) civilization encroaches upon them, they may constitute a national asset of considerable value because they are bright and teachable.

Indian Groups

The Indians inhabiting the lowlands on the other side of the mountains, also are a varied lot. Some of them seem to have stemmed from the Chibchas and speak derivatives of that language. Others speak Quechua, as do the people of the highlands. The majority of coastal Indians live in small villages and are generally easygoing but industrious. In Manabí Province, which is in this area, orginated the world-famed "Panama" hats, made by the Indian and mestizos families in their homes. Today, however, most of the hats for export are made in the highlands, east of the Guayas Estuary, and Cañar and Azuay Provinces.

In the jungles of the northwest Province of Esmeraldas live small groups of semi-savage Indians. Of these the two best-know tribes are the Cayapas and the Colorados. The latter get their name from the fact that they dye their bodies a brilliant red. The dye they use is the juice of *achiote* seeds, which are exported by the ton for coloring foods.

At the southern end of the coastal strip, north of the Guayas Estuary, the coast is dry and sandy, and populated only by seekers after gold and petroleum, and the bones of prehistoric monsters. Here is Ecuador's only oil field, operated by an Anglo-Ecuadorian company, which supplies the country, and the domestic airlines with gasoline, fuel, and lubricants.

Thirty miles up the Guayas Estuary is the beautiful, and mostly modern, town of Guayaquil, commercial center of the country. Although Guayaquil was founded in 1535 by Sebastian Belalcázar, it was sacked by buccaneers, wrecked time and again by earthquakes, and almost entirely destroyed by fire, so that little of the original town remains. From the river it looks like a new and splendid city of magnificant marble buildings and monuments. For a long time it suffered from recurring epidemics of bubonic and yellow fever. But with the help of the Rockefeller Foundation, the flea-ridden rats and the plague spots were eliminated, and Guayaquil became one of the healthiest ports on the tropical coast.

From Cuenca to Quito

South of the Guayas Estuary is an important industrial and commercial region, centering on Cuenca which has a University almost equal to that of Guayaquil. This territory, however, has long suffered from lack of roads and transportation systems, mule trains being largely used to convey goods to river ports. This shortcoming is being remedied, as will be noted later. The people are mostly mestizos, particularly in the 8,000-foot region, with what seems to be an average of one priest to every ten persons. The real highlands, however, are farther north, and the political center of the country, Quito, sprawls in a saucerlike plateau, 9,500 feet above the sea. Although the Equator crosses the country only a few miles north of Quito, the capital city enjoys a cool, mild, and equable climate. The volcano Pichincha (the boiling mountain), which towers over it, has not erupted seriously since Colonial times.

In the valleys north of Quito are a number of important towns, some of which are sizable manufacturing centers. They range in altitude from 8,500 to 10,000 feet, and make everything from bottles to cement. All around them lies the most beautiful and verdant region of Ecuador, with its fields of wheat and maize, and its grazing lands that support excellent breeds of cattle.

Much of this country, and its aborigines with their gay costumes and smiling faces, are just as they were when the Spaniards first saw them. So attractive a people were the Cara Indians—though they put up a tremendous fight before being subdued—that the Inca took one of their women as concubine. By her he had a son who was to become his favorite—Atahualpa. It was Atahualpa's civil war with his half-brother Huascar, that made things easy for the Spaniards. But the Kingdom of Quitú was not taken over without a bloody struggle. Although the Incas had slaughtered the Cayambe, Caranqui, and Otovalo tribes, there were sufficient of them a few generations later to provide stiff opposition for the men of Spain.

These Indians had had their own civilizations which were not far behind that of the Incas, with well-developed social and political institutions. When Sebastian Belalcázar fought his way into Quito in 1533 there was not much left of the town but ashes. Undaunted, the Conquistadors went about founding a new town, the *Villa de San Francisco de Quitú*, in 1534. The displaced Indians gradually filtered back to their home town, and Quito grew so rapidly that in 1541 it was officially declared a city. Magnificent churches and convents were erected, with Indian labor, and the first school was founded for teaching the Indians to read and write.

The lands of the plateaux, meanwhile, were distributed among the leading Spaniards as feudal lords over the local Indians. Many of these early Spaniards were highly educated, and some of them, together with a number of talented priests, produced notable works of art in painting and sculpture. For nearly a decade, pictures and statuary were an important item of export.

For almost fifty years after the first settlement of the country peace reigned in the *Audiencia de Quito*. But the number of criollos was rapidly growing, and, as the native-born attained positions of importance they became increasingly resentful at the preference shown the Spanish-born by the Crown. A sense of nationalism was developing, and matters came to a head in 1592 wen a sales tax was put on all merchandise. It was the Quito City Council that refused to submit, and the populace rioted. When the Spanish government sent troops to punish the leaders, a militia corps was organized to oppose them, and there was talk of secession from Spain.

Other uprisings occurred in 1625, 1734, and 1736, due largely to the rights and privileges extended to the Spaniards and denied the criollos. Even the Spanish and criollo friars in the monasteries quarreled for the same cause, and the common people took sides. In 1765, the revolt flared into open rebellion. The Spanish officials were ejected, and a criollo leader elected.

The Birth of Independence

One of the prime movers in this beginning struggle for Independence was a true American, Francisco Javier Eugenio de Santa Cruz y Espejo. He was born in Quito of a mulatto mother by a Cajamarcan Indian father. The writings of this man sowed the seeds of Independence that spread throughout the viceroyalty of New Granada, of which Quito was a part at that time. When the Jesuits were expelled, their book collections became public libraries, and Santa Cruz was the first public librarian. His idea was that all Spanish-American Colonies should be separated from the Crown, and become independent republics. He suggested that the colonies work closely together to this end, and that only Americans be permitted to participate in the new governments. He insisted that the clergy, too, must be natives of the colonies, and that the Pope be requested to hand over all excess Church assets for other good works. Not till 1809, long after Santa Cruz's death, did the country achieve independence. Twice in the next few years they lost that independence, and not till 1822 did it become finally assured by the victory of General Antonio José de Sucre at Pichincha.

Ecuador, at this time, was part of Greater Colombia, from which it seceded in 1830 to become an independent nation. But, like its neighbors, Ecuador did not find peace with freedom and sovereignty. There were recurring clashes between the rival towns of Quito and Guayaquil, and between personalities in government circles. Educated mestizos bore the brunt of the battle in the fight for independence, but they did not extend its privileges to their humbler brethren. For a long time, the vote was restricted to those literates who owned property or belonged to the professions. Even today, the vast majority of the people never learn to read so that the illiterates total 43.7%. They live close to the soil, as they have done since time immemorial, weaving cloth to make their clothes, manufacturing thick felt to make their hats, and raising their own food on small plots. The independent Indians of the Sierras, who were decimated but not conquered by the Incas, dye their clothes with gay colors and make their own music. At their frequent fairs and fiestas they are as carefree and jolly—and often as drunk—as if they did not know the meaning of ignorance and oppression.

Bridges, Rails, Roads—a New Epoch

Within the last few decades attempts have been made to extend the facilities for public education, but little could be done to improve the economic status of the Indians until the national income was increased and transportation simplified. Until quite recently the principal railroad was that running from Guayaquil to Quito, a distance of 288 miles, and ninety miles beyond. Scattered short lines on the coast and in the south totalled perhaps another 250 miles. Roads were more extensive within limited areas but the poor condition of some of them precluded year-round travel. In the Pacific coastal area the roads were often mere trails and haulage was effected by mules and llamas. In the past ten years, however, tremendous strides have been taken in opening up the country. The railroad from Quito to Esmeraldas was finally completed in 1956, and a program of highways linking the plateaux with the coastal areas launched. Hotels and airports have been improved, and the Port of Guayaquil modernized, with a bridge across the Guayas River projected.

The only two Pacific coast ports worth mentioning are Esmeraldas and Manta. The country's one important port is Guayaquil, and the Guayas River forms the principal highway into the interior. Down it float rafts of balsa logs to the lumber yards, rafts bearing tons of cacao beans and vegetable ivory (tagua nuts), while scores of eager motor boats convey passengers and goods to and from the upriver port of Babahoya and other small towns.

Though very few products that come from the plateaux are destined for export, there is a healthy traffic in manufactured goods for home consumption. Most of the industries are established in the mountain regions where there is hydroelectric power available from some of the many rivers. In the lowlands are the sugar mills, the cacao, coffee, and banana plantations, and the petroleum refineries. This makes a system of rapid and cheap transportation highly desirable, but the topography has hitherto rendered it difficult of attainment. The one railroad from the lowlands to the highlands cost around $73,000 a mile thirty years ago. With the growing availability of petroleum fuels there is a possibility of increasing manufactures in the coastal areas.

Cacao was for long the principal export item, but a

disease that struck the plantations in the 1920s almost ruined the planters and recovery has been desperately slow. Today the exports of cacao form only 14 per cent of the total. Bananas are now the major export (55%), with coffee a low second at 24%.

Industry in Ecuador seems to employ about fifteen thousand workers and, strangely enough, the Indians and mestizos of the towns who compose the unskilled and semi-skilled labor are unusually adept at mastering the details of mechanical processes.

In the highlands, where a great many of the Indians and mestizos live in self-contained communities, most of the land is held by the small white aristocracy. The laborers work under overseers, producing wheat, corn, barley, quinoa, beans, potatoes, lentils, and other vegetables. Cattle are pastured in the higher elevations, either on the grassy paramos or in the alfalfa fields. But in most cases methods are crude. The plowman still uses a sharpened stick pulled by an ox, and cultivated with a hoe. The use of fertilizers, and the principles of crop rotation are practically unknown. At harvest time the grain is trodden out by oxen and winnowed by hand. Production per acre therefore is low.

On the other hand, the average Indian or mestizo lives fairly comfortably and without too many privations. He has a warm hut of sundried brick with a tile or straw roof, and his wife makes his clothes from cloth she weaves and dyes herself. These women it seems are never idle. As they go back and forth to market they twirl a distaff in one hand to make the wool or cotton thread. Altogether they are far more advanced than the lowlands Indians, and give promise of some day developing into a worthwhile middle class if ever they are given a chance to learn and progress as their forefathers did five hundred years before. But when that day comes Ecuador will lose much of its color and charm for the visitor from abroad.

Meanwhile, however, the country is progressing to an astonishing degree, thanks to almost continuous political stability since 1944, accompanied by statesmanlike handling of the country's economy. With the $5,000,000 trade surplus achieved in 1957 (in spite of the "Panama" hat trade being in the doldrums), and the opening up of the country through new and better communications facilities which make possible industrial development, the future of Ecuador seems bright indeed.

P E R U

PERU:

CHAPTER 12

INCAN HERITAGE

IN ALL OF SOUTH AMERICA, NO OLD-time civilization ever attained greater heights than that of early Peru. First in the Tiahuanacos, and then the Incan Empire, the aboriginal Indians proved their capacity for rapid and tremendous progress in the arts, in government, and in engineering. Then came the Spanish treasure-hunters and in a few short years, all that the Incas had so carefully organized and created over the centuries was destroyed and its people reduced to abject serfdom. The artisans who designed and made the beautiful ornaments of gold were set to digging that metal out of the hills; the granaries and irrigation systems were destroyed, and the cultivators of the land were slaves to new masters who thought only of riches and overlooked famine.

The treasure of gold and silver that it had taken the Incas centuries to accumulate, went to fatten the purses and paunches of the conquistadors, the priests and parasites, and swell the coffers of the Royal House of Spain. To appease this insatiable thirst for riches, the mines were worked and the river gravels panned, without thought for the human minds and bodies that were sacrificed in the process. Indian life was cheap, and the millions of heathen souls rapidly dwindled to a few hundred thousand. Today, the descendants of these Incan tribes constitute about forty-six per cent of the country's 9,651,000 population, and their mestizo sons and daughters slightly more (53%). Of the civilization that they created little is left, and the people as a whole are far worse off than they were four hundred years ago.

Incan Social Strata

It is not easy to appraise the Inca culture from the viewpoint of its people, but it seems clear from this distance, that even the poorest and most humble of them were infinitely better off under the Incas, even though their civilization was not one that we would wish to emulate today. Spain and the rest of the Old World had cultures based on class distinctions. The Inca civilization, too, had its classes, but it was a step ahead of the rest of the world because it did not permit its poor to starve. The Incan social strata consisted of the Inca himself and those of royal blood; next in rank were the heads of the tribes subject to the Incas, then the landholding peasants, and the artisans, and below them the servants of the ruling classes and the shepherds and workers on their lands.

Monogamy was enforced in the case of the lower classes, but the Inca and the nobles had both wives and large numbers of concubines. And although they treated most of the children of these unions as bastards, and gave them no privileges, the fact remains that they were unwittingly, raising the quality of the Incan stock. This large-scale intermarriage between the Incas and the subject tribes also tended to unify the empire, and produce a people that had uniform characteristics. The general trend, therefore, was upward, and, given a few more centuries, it is pretty certain that a generally superior race would have developed in Peru. But the Spaniards killed off the leaders and reduced the common people to slavery which only the wit-dulling habit of coca-chewing made bearable.

A great deal of confusion and uncertainty exists as to how many people lived in Peru when the Spaniards arrived. Some say eight, ten, fifteen, or even twenty millions composed the Incan Empire, but all these figures seem ridiculously high when we estimate the amount of agricultural produce that would have been necessary to support them. Modern Peru has about seventeen million acres of land in pasture and less than four million acres given over to crops in the area that was occupied by the Incas. With all their irrigation systems it seems impossible that they could have cultivated more than the four million acres.

Careful calculations have shown that each million persons would need 433,300 acres to support them. Since the people undoubtedly did not live on an exclusive diet of maize, much of the land must have been used for other crops. Furthermore a large percentage of the land was not cultivated every year, but allowed to lie fallow.

This means that somewhere between two and three million acres of land must have been in cultivation constantly. Since it would, on the basis of these estimates, have taken about one and a quarter million acres to support a million persons, the population of Peru at this time could not have exceeded two millions or so.

That this should be so is suggested by the recorded fact that many of the Spaniards had insufficient Indians to cultivate their lands. When the country was first split up among the conquerors, each Spaniard of any consequence had anywhere from a few dozen to thousands of Indians to work for him. Pizarro himself claimed 100,000, but his commanders and governors were nowhere near so fortunate. The Indians, it seems, died faster than they bred.

With the Spaniards doing their best to rectify the situation by increasing the birth rate, the numbers of mestizos multiplied rapidly as the Indians declined. Actually, there were more Spaniards than there was land to support them, and many thousands of them had to do without estates of any kind or size. Some of them became so poor that they had to go and live among the Indians, where they at least would get something to eat.

In 1574, there were 160,000 Spaniards in Peru, but only four thousand of them owned land and Indians to work it. These inequalities were largely responsible for the series of civil wars that raged between the Spaniards from 1538 to 1554. Those landowners who had no claim to profits from the mines began to develop the agricultural resources of their estates. From Spain they brought all kinds of fruit, vegetables, and livestock. Vineyards and orange groves were planted, and wines were an important product before 1600. The biggest export crop at this time was sugar, though sheep were bred in enormous numbers, and their wool shipped to Spain in large quantities.

Coastal Rivers and Oases

The limited amount of useful land in Peru was due, as it is today, to the dry climate of the coast, and the rocky mountainous nature of the interior. The thousands of square miles east of the Andes were added to Peruvian territory at a much later date, and even now are of little practical value. The 1,400-mile coastal strip was then, as now, practically all desert, the mountains coming down to within eighty miles of the ocean. The whole stretch, fortunately, is not entirely unproductive. No less than fifty-two rivers coming down from the mountains create narrow, fertile valleys, enabling this ten per cent of the country to support about a third of the nine-and-a-half million population.

In the old days, each of these valleys, or groups of valleys, had its own distinct culture. Most of the desert is at 8,000 feet altitude between the coastal mountains and the high Andes, so that the heat is not always too much for human endurance. Much of the time this area is swept by cool sea breezes, chilled by the Humboldt current which robs them of their moisture. In the valleys, today, are the most important towns, and manufacturing centers, and, in the northern desert are the most productive oil wells of the Pacific coast.

In sharp contrast with this area is the Sierra region, where two thirds of the people live. This was the area from which the riches came that drew the Conquistadors, and the people went on living there after that feverish activity had died down. The mines were in the western range of the Andes, some of whose peaks reach 22,000 feet into the blue. Between this and the eastern range is a confusion of ridges, valleys, and plateaux. Large areas suitable for agriculture lie at altitudes of over ten thousand feet.

At the southern end is Lake Titicaca, which Peru shares with Bolivia, and around it are excellent farming lands. Toward the north, the rivers which run north and south have cut deep valleys. In these sheltered spots, where the altitude is not more than five thousand feet, the climate is almost tropical, and here sugar cane and rice are grown. In this mountain area, between Bolivia and Ecuador, almost every kind of climate is found, and extreme differences exist within short distances. The individual areas of arable land, together with adequate water supplies for irrigation are limited, and the Indians cultivate them intensively to supply local needs. In the higher elevations, every available patch of grazing land is given over to sheep and llamas.

The Copper Mines

Differences in land ownership and operation vary almost as much as the climates. Some of it is held in large haciendas, and in other areas the Indians have become associated in group organizations that own the land collectively. In still other instances, individual Indian families own small plots of land of their own. In the central part of the western cordillera are the modern copper mines which replaced the silver mines of the Incas. These mines are at elevations of over 14,000 feet, and production is handicapped by difficulties of transporation. The labor is supplied by Indians who are used to heavy exertion at such altitudes.

The refining plants are usually located a couple of thousand feet below the mines, and their presence has given rise to a peculiar situation. The fumes from the smelters kill all vegetation for miles around, and this has been disastrous for a large number of Indian families living in the vicinity of the plants. To compensate these people for the loss of their livelihood, the copper companies, at the request of the Peruvian Government, agreed to supply the Indians with food. Many of these people, however, prefer to move to other locations.

Silver is still produced in important quantities in this region, together with a variety of other metals including vanadium, in which the country has a virtual monopoly. Less than five per cent of Peru's people live on the eastern flanks of the Andes where there is little but rain jungle through which flow hundreds of shallow rivers on their way to the Amazon or its main extension, the Marañon. There is but one large center of population in this area, the Amazon port of Iquitos, where ninety per cent of the people are Indians.

Located twenty three hundred miles from the mouth of the Amazon, Iquitos can be reached by ocean-going vessels of moderate draft. Originally an important port during the rubber boom at the turn of the century, the town is still important as an outlet for balata gum, rubber, cotton, and tobacco, all emanating from parts of Peru difficult of access from the Pacific ports. There is now a highway from Lima over the Andes to Pucallpa on the Ucayali River, along which passengers and goods from the coast can be brought down the Ucayali River on small boats to be transhipped at Iquitos. Other small river settlements exist in the eastern jungles, but most of the Indians live undisturbed in the forests, and take no part in the economic life of the nation.

Shifting Populations

One important effect of the sixteenth century invasion was the redistribution of the population. In these early days the valleys were heavily populated; Cuzco was the only town of any size or importance, the rest of the people being scattered over the agricultural and pastoral lands, living in small villages or towns that had no particular form or arrangement. The Spaniards quickly built up towns from one end of Peru to the other, many of them in regions that previously had little population. The City of Lima, for example, was planted in a spot where no town had existed before, and soon had a greater population than the Inca capital of Cuzco.

Hundreds of thousands of Indians were sent to the mines of Potosí (in modern Bolivia), and Huancavelica. As the Spaniards drove back the Araucanian Indians, they freed useful lands which they settled. These immigrations resulted in the abandonment of hitherto populated areas, together with the irrigation works, so that whole regions reverted to wasteland and desert.

The Indians, unaccustomed to long and arduous work in the mines at high altitudes, died off in large numbers, and the living conditions in populous centers gave rise to epidemics which also took a heavy toll of life. Nevertheless, when the necessity for increased agricultural activity grew, the Indians began to increase in numbers again, and, until quite recent times, when the mestizos forged ahead, have constituted a majority of the population.

The Jesuit Missions

East of the Andes the Jesuit missions became active along the Marañon River in the early 17th century. By 1653 they claimed control over 15,000 families of jungle Indians. But in the next hundred years, many of the Indians changed their minds, and retired to their jungle fastnesses. Many who did not were shanghaied by Brazilian slave raiders, and the Church's brown peons were reduced to a mere 15,000 individuals. The good that the Jesuits may have done was soon obliterated in this area. In other parts of Peru, the Jesuits took a leading part in promoting colonial commerce and manufactures. As the Spanish and criollo population grew, there grew with it a demand for more and more products of Spain. But in most cases, such things as fabrics and clothing were prohibitively high in cost by the time they reached Peru.

The idea in Spain was to keep the colony dependent upon the mother country for most manufactured goods, and to control production of all commodities for the benefit of Spanish manufacturers and traders. But, as some of the early viceroys discovered, this was not wholly practical because Spain could not supply all the colony required and compromises had to be effected.

Caciques *in Industry*

An extraordinary feature of conditions in Peru was that the Indian caciques (chiefs) were allowed to employ native labor for the manufacture of cloth and other things for domestic consumption without regulation. At this time it was customary to segregate the Indians in the various communities, and this left them at the mercy of their own leaders who had little more consideration for them than the Spaniards had.

In spite of all trade regulations and laws designed to protect the Indians, the colony went pretty much its own way, and business and industry soon began to flourish. Woolen and cotton textiles were made throughout the territory of the former Incan Empire, particularly in the Quito area. This soon spread south as far as Chile. Large numbers of Peruvian Indians were engaged in handicrafts in fabrics, leather, silver, etc. during the 18th century. Few of them, however, were able to better their position or acquire even moderate wealth because the people who made the money were the middlemen or traders.

One of the most important results of the Spanish rule, insofar as the Indians were concerned, was the rapid changing of an agricultural population into a nation of wage earners without land or other possessions. Under the Incas, every man was assured of subsistence, and money was unnecessary. Under the Spaniards, a large portion of the people could grow nothing for themselves, and were dependent upon what they could buy or trade, or were given by their masters. They were, legally, considered as free men, a doubtful benefit since in the majority of cases they were no better than "debt slaves," perpetually owing their employer and unable to leave him or get better terms elsewhere until that debt was discharged. In this, of course, they were no worse off than millions of others in Europe at this period of the world's history.

This, then, was the manner in which the country developed. The Incas had split up each conquered tribe, transporting groups of these new subjects to various parts of the country so that they would be more quickly absorbed into the general population. The Spaniards not only mixed them up further, but added a growing percentage of children of mixed blood, most of whom lived with their mothers as Indians. In a couple of centuries, therefore, the native population was more unified in character, more homogeneous, than it had ever been. Yet within it there was soon to grow a large class of landless workers; wage-earners in trade and industry.

Above the Indian and mestizo masses were the descendants of the Indian caciques and their families, and other Indian and mestizo individuals who had been in a position to acquire wealth and property. These formed the basis of a slowly developing middle class, the shopkeepers, tradesmen and artisans. These mestizos who were acknowledged by their Spanish fathers, or whose parents actually were married, multiplied rapidly in numbers and took over increasingly important positions in the Colonial government. Eventually, since they owned most of the country's wealth, they became the dominant social group, the Colonial aristocracy, along with the criollos of pure Spanish blood.

Little occurred in Colonial days to change this trend, but there was a gradually awakening realization on the part of the landowners, large and small, as to the necessity for increasing the volume of agricultural products.

The First President

The independence of Peru was proclaimed in 1821, and a president elected, but not until the battle of Ayacucho, in 1824, was the country freed from Spanish domination. Even then it took another year to drive the last of the Spanish forces from the port of Callao, and finally assure the independence of South America. The Liberator, Simon Bolívar, was elected President of the new republic, but he proved to be a better soldier than a statesman. In 1828 he was replaced by General de Lamar, and the first Constitution was written a year later. This launched a struggle for power among the various political personalities that kept the country in a turmoil for the next twenty years.

In 1829, Peru went to war with Colombia, in the first of its interminable boundary disputes, and Lamar was deposed. In 1835, the Bolivian dictator, Santa Cruz, intervened to form the Peru-Bolivia confederation. Chile and Argentina objected to this and Chile started hostilities which resulted in the confederation being dissolved in 1839.

Guano and Nitrates

Meanwhile, the more accessible mines of Peru were becoming exhausted, and in looking for substitute sources of wealth, the Peruvians turned to the nitrate beds of Tarapacá, their most southerly province, and to the *guano* deposits on the islands off the coast. This guano consists of vast beds of bird droppings that have accumulated from time immemorial. The Humboldt current, sweeping up the coast from the Antarctic, brings with it enormous quantities of animal and plant life. This rich store of food attracts millions of small fish. The fish, in turn, serve as food for myriad birds. These birds live on the chain of desert islands that stretch 850 miles along the Peruvian coast, and leave their tremendous amounts of nitrogenous material so valuable as a fertilizer.

The Peruvians began to exploit these guano beds on a large scale in 1840, and they supplied the bulk of the national income for the next forty years. This enabled the government to spend considerable sums on the irrigation of new agricultural areas, and build both highways and railroads of which the country was in sore need. This period of prosperity attracted large numbers of immigrants, including many Negroes and orientals. Slavery, meanwhile, had been abolished in 1855.

During this same period, the nitrate beds were developed to some degree. Both Bolivia and Chile were working their own nitrate deposits at this time, and when they fell out, in 1879, Peru was dragged into the war against Chile through a previous agreement with Bolivia. The result of this military adventure was disastrous for Peru. The country not only lost all of its nitrate desert, but the guano islands, the city of Lima, and other important areas were occupied by Chile. In 1893, Chile withdrew, leaving Peru practically bankrupt. In order to secure foreign loans, which were desperately needed to revive her trade, Peru had to grant concessions, giving her creditors control over her major resources, including the guano deposits, mines, railways, and farmlands. Subsequent revolutions kept the country in a state of political instability until early in the twentieth century.

Copper, Cotton and Sugar

In spite of all these setbacks, important new industries were established and old ones expanded. Within a few years, the Republic was once again on a firm economic foundation. The discovery of high-grade copper lodes, the extension of cotton growing areas through irrigation, and the planting of large new areas with sugar cane, built up a valuable export business. Later, the finding of petroleum in the northern desert added another export commodity that quickly exceeded all others in dollar value.

The opening of the Panama Canal helped the country considerably, and with a growing prosperity, the leading cities and towns were able materially to raise the standard of living of their inhabitants. Good water supplies and sewerage systems were introduced, and electric lighting made almost universally available.

The buying power of the people in the towns was increased, but the vast majority of the Indian and mestizo workers were little affected. This applies particularly to the farm laborers on the great haciendas, who are little better off today than they were four hundred years ago. Their brethren who work in the mines—some 35,000 of them—are considerably better off both in wages and the freedom to change their jobs if they don't like them.

Not so well paid but more healthfully employed are the 30,000 toilers in the sugar fields, and the smaller number employed in building roads and other public works by the Government. This still leaves a substantial number that have their own small farms, some of which produce considerably more than they consume. The sheep farms of the highlands give employment to some thousands more who have little to be thankful for beyond the bare necessities of life. The middle class is small and confined to the towns, although some of the 25,000 Japanese are small farmers who keep pretty much to themselves.

Both increased prosperity and the spread of education among the poor have long been limited by the lack of transportation facilities throughout the country. As a result schools are scarce and illiteracy high. The terrain does not lend itself to the building of either railways or roads, but it appears that something is to be done about this. Though the country generally faces difficult times due to a falling off in demand for its zinc, lead, and copper, foreign companies are going ahead with their projects. The most important of these is the development of copper deposits in Southern Peru, a project that will employ thousands. Another concern is to tunnel the high Andes and divert water to operate a 240,000-kilowatt hydro-electric plant. This same project will increase the water supply for rapidly growing Lima, and irrigate 20,000 acres of land. Oil exploration in the jungle regions of the Oriente is being stepped up, and the iron ore deposits 400 miles south of Lima will be developed. Largely with government money, a new airport is to be constructed for jet liners, and a $75,000,000 highway project launched, and several ports modernized.

All these things suggest a faith in the future of Peru by other nationals—a faith that its natural resources and potentialities seem to justify. The only unknown quantity would seem to be time.

V E N E Z U E L A

CHAPTER 13

VENEZUELA: VENICE ON THE CARIBBEAN

WHEN ALONSO DE OJEDA SAILED INTO Lake Maracaibo in 1499, and found Indians living in houses built on stilts in the water, he called the place Venezuela—Little Venice! The huts are still there; otherwise the country bears little resemblance to anything in Europe. Today it is a country of six million people and the lake is littered with oil derricks mounted on piles from which spouts the black gold that makes the republic the most prosperous of all nations on the continent.

In the early days of the conquest, Venezuela had little to recommend it. The adjacent island of Margarita, which was headquarters for pirates and slave traders, in 1510 turned out to be the site of some of the richest pearl fisheries in history. But so avidly were the waters fished that within a few years there was nothing left. The pirates, however, continued to sell slaves to the islands, and many a Spaniard was able to buy a winsome Indian girl of thirteen for a couple of hatchets, and sell her for a hundred pesos on the island. But most of them were after bigger game than this.

In 1520, activities were transferred to the mainland, and the first European settlement in South America was founded—the town of Cumuná. Excursions into the neighboring country failed to turn up any gold or other treasure, and the Spaniards moved farther west in 1527 to a place they called Santa Ana de Coro.

With Coro as a base, the Spaniards sent out a number of gold-hunting expeditions, both by river and land. Their persistence was finally rewarded when, after butchering and torturing of a large number of Indians, they plunged into the valley of Lake Valencia. The Lake Valencia basin proving to be a rich highlands agricultural area, the conquistadors established the town of Valencia there, and put slave Indians to work planting crops. From this point they moved on eastward into the equally fertile, but much more easily defendable valley of Caracas and founded the capital city of that name.

The Welsers and the Fuggers

Meanwhile, strange things were happening in Spain. King Charles V had gained the crown of the Holy Roman Empire, and almost bankrupted himself in doing it. The tide of treasure had not yet begun to flow from the New World and Charles was in desperate need of funds. He was ready to borrow money from anyone, and give anything or everything as security. To the King of Portugal he pledged the Spice Islands (the Moluccas) for 350,000 ducats; to the German bankers, the Fuggers, he offered the rights to Chile, and to the Welsers he handed Venezuela.

At this distance it seems incredible that a group of hard-headed bankers would hand over vast sums in cash for territory of dubious worth. It later transpired that these shrewd financiers had not only heard whispers of the almost limitless treasure that would soon be on its way to the king from Mexico, and expected to find the same in South America, but their cupidity had been aroused by tales of El Dorado. Venezuela was the logical place from which to launch expeditions in search of the fabled golden king.

This was the reason that in the early 1500s the few Spaniards in Venezuela found themselves pushed aside by the ravenous agents of the Welsers. The Germans quickly showed their determination to secure a substantial return on their investment regardless of all moral considerations. They had no spiritual ideals to restrain them, and no duty to Christianize the Indians. If the Spaniards were cruel, the Germans were ruthless and inhuman. At each fresh disappointment, they avenged themselves on the Indians, burning them in their huts and villages. In their mad obsession they took no time to found settlements or lay out towns. The fate of their one expedition to the El Dorado of the Chibchas, was related in connection with the story of Colombia. After twenty-six years of bloody terror, which earned for them even the detestation of the Spaniards, they abandoned their worthless empire and went back to prison or poverty, with nothing to show for their pains but a parrot or two.

Raleigh and El Dorado

From 1555 on, the Spaniards had Venezuela to themselves. But the Germans did leave behind a number of fantastic tales to whet the appetites of explorers and treasure hunters to come. One, Ambrosius Ehinger, averred that he had discovered the rich country of the Amazons, first mentioned by that ardent traveller, Marco Polo, two centuries before. Nicholaus Federmann, foiled in his attempt to find El Dorado on the Sabana de Bogotá, invented a fabulous city of pygmies. These, however, were poor substitutes for the persistent tales of El Dorado—the mysterious city of gold, that now had bobbed up in Venezuela. The Germans no longer had a stomach for such ventures, but in England, Sir Walter Raleigh swallowed the fantastic myth, hook, line and sinker! El Dorado had now become the golden city of Manoa, where the Incas, fleeing from Pizarro, had taken their treasure. The city they had built alongside a lake called Parimé, in the wilds of Venezuela, and the only way to reach it was, supposedly, by a long journey up the Orinoco River.

Cutting the wide llanos (plains) of Venezuela in two, the 1,700-mile-long Orinoco empties into the Atlantic through a score of mouths.

In 1595, ten years after he had founded the colony of Virginia, Raleigh sailed on his first expedition to this unknown river. Between then and 1617, he made three trips in search of El Dorado, and each time returned empty-handed. He even failed to discover the tribe of weird beings he had described in a letter to the Queen—the headless people whose eyes were in their shoulders, and their mouths in the middle of their chests. He did make friends with the Indians, but found them indifferent when he tried to arouse them against the Spaniards. They had not yet suffered as their people had who came in contact with the Welsers. On the way home, Raleigh dropped in at Cumuná, and set fire to the town when the inhabitants refused to supply his expedition with food.

By this time the Spaniards had half-heartedly begun to settle the country and develop its agricultural resources. They had built the cities of Maracaibo on the Gulf (1571), Barquesimeto in the coastal highlands (1552), a port at La Guaira (1588), and several smaller towns. They had begun the importation of considerable numbers of Negro slaves, and had difficulty in quelling them when they staged an uprising in 1550. Cattle were introduced in 1548, together with a large number of vegetables, fruits, and cereals.

Within a few years, the country was producing extensive crops of corn, potatoes, wheat, bananas, and sugar. Later on, cacao and tobacco were added in exportable quantities. Thus, although the country was comparatively neglected by the treasure hunters, it did achieve some importance in supplying other Caribbean settlements, and a number of islands, with foodstuffs the Conquistadors were too preoccupied to grow for themselves. Furthermore, being a thousand miles nearer Spain than Panamá, it formed a useful re-provisioning depot for the treasure ships both homeward and outward bound.

So promising did the future commercial development of the country seem in the 17th century, that for a period its commerce was taken over by a trading organization called the Biscayan Merchants Association. But there were problems even in those days, due to the difficulties of the terrain.

The country actually consists of four strongly contrasting areas—the hot lowland strip around "Lake" Maracaibo which is an almost landlocked arm of the Caribbean; the northern highlands, formed by an arm of the Andes that stretches around the lake and eastward along the Caribbean coast; the vast llanos (plains) sweeping in a wide arc from the Colombian border to the Atlantic, and the comparatively unknown Orinoco delta and the neighboring Guiana highlands.

The original inhabitants of Venezuela had consisted of both Arawak and Carib Indians. A large proportion of these had been massacred or otherwise wiped out in the occupied areas. But once the country was more or less settled, the population was augmented by substantial numbers of mestizos and zambos and a few mulattoes. On the plains, the Indians, like the Guaranís of Argentina, took to the horses that were then running wild. They and their mestizo sons soon became expert horsemen, and later were an important factor in the struggle for independence. For the time being, however, they were content to use their skill in the saddle for the purpose of building up a business in cattle hides.

Savage Motilones

On the western borders of the country, the savage Motilones Indians of the Sierra de Perijá, were the chief thorn in the flesh of Spaniards and Indians alike. Time and again these low-grade primitives destroyed settlements and missions. They are, incidentally, just as irreconcilable today. In recent years, when an oil company began opening up a field on the Colombian border, the workers had to wear shirts of chain mail to protect them from the arrows of these savages. The rail wagons they used in laying tracks through the jungle were provided with high sides of corrugated iron for the same purpose. In spite of such precautions, many an engineer and laborer was badly hurt or foully murdered. The activities of these Motilones actually kept the Spaniards from settling a considerable area for a long time. Even today, that section is lightly populated.

Farther north, at the mouth of the Maracaibo lake, live an equally interesting but far more peaceable group of Indians. These are the Goajiras, who had an agricultural civilization, before taking up cattle raising, and became extremely useful to the Spaniards in more ways than one. Today they are a valuable element in the population. Many of them settled in the villages and agricultural areas around the lake, the men taking up various trades or becoming laborers, while a large number of women entered domestic service in the city of Maracaibo.

The four diverse regions inhabited by these Indians differed greatly in their products, and suffered from a lack of unity due to difficulties of access and communication. It is therefore not surprising that they also developed political antagonisms, as a result of which armed clashes between the various localities whose interests differed were common throughout Venezuelan history. This was but one other factor that delayed the advancement of the country.

In the early days, the few cattle turned loose on the llanos multiplied enormously, much to the delight of the plains Indians, but, as an industry, cattle raising suffered from lack of easy access to ports, and moreover, was subjected to the same severe restrictions that Spain imposed on all commerce. As an example of the aggravating stupidity of such laws, after 1777, the growth of tobacco was restricted, and Venezuelans were compelled to smuggle Brazilian tobacco into the country, for their own use.

Having to work hard for a living, with no possibility

of uncovering rich treasure, the colonists were never in any mood to submit to repression, and smuggling, with the aid of several European countries, antagonistic to Spain, was, for a long time, their most thriving activity. Under such unhealthy conditions, it is not surprising that agitation for a republic was rife by 1796.

Miranda and Bolívar

In spite of Venezuela's comparative insignificance in the minds of the early Spaniards, it was there that the seeds of independence were first sown. Here were born two of the great liberators, Miranda and Bolívar. The third was San Martín of Argentina. Venezuela was also one of the countries to suffer most in the long and bloody struggle that followed the declaration of independence. Miranda served in the French contingent of the American Continental Army from 1779 to 1781. This experience inspired him to work actively for the liberation of South America, and he spent the next twenty years travelling through Europe and Russia seeking military and financial aid.

In 1806, Miranda secured the backing of some New York merchants, and set sail with a fleet of three ships manned by adventurers, to take over Venezuela. Surprised by Spanish coastguard ships off Trinidad, Miranda's ship, the Leander, made off, leaving the others to their fate. The crews of these ships, and everyone else aboard, Spaniards and Americans alike, were promptly hanged, and their heads exposed on pikes as a warning to others. Undaunted, Miranda raided the Venezuela coast and actually captured the town of Coro, but, much to his astonishment, the inhabitants were actually hostile, and he had to withdraw.

The trouble was that in this neglected colony, there were few Spanish officials, and the Spanish population was small. The mestizos and Indians either were satisfied with things as they were or they could see no benefit to them by official separation from Spain. It was therefore up to the leading Spaniards to take the initiative. One of these was Simon Bolívar, son of a wealthy landowner, who was to become known throughout South America as The Great Liberator.

Following his education in Europe, Bolívar had witnessed the final scenes of the French Revolution. In Italy he was present when Napoleon placed the iron crown of the Lombards on his own head. On the Aventine, in Rome, Bolívar pledged his life to the liberation of his country. Independence was declared in 1811.

First with Miranda, then alone, Bolívar suffered smashing defeats. In 1812, the Spaniards had regained Venezuela, and the white men languished in the dungeons of LaGuaira, chained to the Negroes whose equality they had proclaimed. But Bolívar had been allowed to depart; he was not considered of sufficient importance to detain! Soon he was back, this time to join the rebels in New Granada. Given a small command there, he destroyed the Spanish outposts along the Magdalena, climbed over the Andes, and plunged through the torrid jungles of the lowlands. Killing without mercy, and taking no prisoners, he entered Caracas in triumph. But Caracas was already a city of mourning. A devastating earthquake had rent the country, killing 10,000 in Caracas alone.

Then came the struggle that decimated the population of Venezuela and ended in Bolívar's flight. His adversary in this bloody struggle was a Spanish storekeeper with a following of savage *llaneros,* who had an unpleasant custom of decorating their hats with their enemies' ears. Shopkeeper Boves soon became known as the Tiger of the Plains.

In this war of extermination almost a quarter of a million of the people of Caracas Province were slain. Less than half of them were left to flee with Bolívar to the wilds. Bolívar's cousin, José Felix Ribas, seized command of the remnants of the army as Boves died from his wounds. The llaneros avenged their leader by decapitating Ribas, frying his head, and sticking it on a lance to parade with it through the streets of Caracas. But Bolívar was not yet beaten, even though ten thousand troops under the Spanish General Pablo Morillo had arrived to crush the revolution.

Bolívar in Haiti

In black Haiti he found a friend. Haiti at this time, was divided into a republic under Alexander Pétion, a Negro blacksmith, and a kingdom ruled by Henri-Christophe. Pétion not only offered Bolívar sanctuary, but placed at his disposal a small army of blacks. With these Negroes, and a small handful of whites, Bolívar again invaded Venezuela, and the only reward Pétion would accept was Bolívar's promise that all black slaves would be freed. Bolívar displayed his feelings toward the blacks by inducing his sister to marry one of his Negro generals.

With the help of the llaneros, now organized on the side of the republic by José Antonio Páez, Bolívar now marched on from one triumph to another. The conquest of Venezuela ended on the banks of the Orinoco, in the battle of Carabobo. From Angostura, for ever after to be called Ciudad Bolívar, he set out with his ragged army of mestizos, Negroes, mulattos, Indians and whites, many wearing straw hats and armed only with sticks, to conquer, with the help of the British legion, the rest of the continent in the name of independence.

But Venezuela was exhausted and its population reduced by almost twenty-five per cent. Of its four and a half million cattle at the beginning of the struggle, a meager two hundred and fifty thousand remained, with scarcely a sufficient number of llaneros to take care of them. With the end of the war, the internal political strife began, accentuated by the differences between the contrasting regions and the aims and needs of their people. Progress was impossible, and not till the country seceded from Greater Colombia in 1830 did trade begin to pick up.

By the middle of the nineteenth century, coffee, sugar, cacao were being exported in sizeable quantities, and the herds of cattle were approaching their former size. An era of political calm descended upon the country with the presidency of Antonio Guzmán Blanco in 1870, and the country prospered for the next twenty years. Roads and railroads were built, telegraphs installed, and, what is equally important, there was an awakening of interest in the arts and education. Church was separated from State, and all religions tolerated.

Gómez Takes Over

The spell was broken in 1896 when a civil war began that lasted two years. Political meddling got the government into arguments with Britain, Germany, and Italy, and warships blockaded the ports. Civil disturbances continued to put a brake on economic progress till 1910 when the greatest of Venezuela's dictators, General Juan Vicente Gómez, took the reins. This ruthless tyrant mercilessly suppressed all opposition, hanging troublemakers like butcher's meat from hooks. But he did restore internal peace and economic stability. In the thirty-six years of his iron rule he brought prosperity to the country, and himself. And though he never married, he gave his country more than eighty lusty infants bearing his name. When he died in 1935, at the age of 77, he was still concerned with finding a perfect mother for a legitimate son whom he might make his heir!

Population and Prospects Today

The whole economic condition of the country was changed by the discovery of oil in worthwhile quantities in 1920, and its large-scale exploitation begun in 1921. This oil was found in the Maracaibo Basin, in such quantities that the country rapidly became the third largest producer in the world (after the USA and Russia), and the world's greatest exporter of petroleum products. This vast production was made possible only by calling in foreign capital and foreign engineers. Though the country as a whole benefited from the heavy taxes on this oil, the country's new wealth did little to help the living conditions of the poor. As a matter of fact, living costs even today are so high in Venezuela that the poor man has a hard time making ends meet.

The position of the oil industry in the overall picture

of Venezuela's economy, is perhaps best judged by a review of modern conditions in that country as related to population distribution, and regional physiographic and climatic conditions. The lowlands bordering Lake Maracaibo are one of the hottest regions in the Continent, the average temperatures of around 80 degrees being accompanied by high humidity in the southern end, and aridity in the north. This is the wealthiest portion of Venezuela, with its oil at the Caribbean end and fertile lowland plains occupied by sugar and cacao plantations. Thick rain forests cover the lower end of the basin, providing a rich variety of forest products. Maracaibo City in the north is the chief center of population in this area, and in the semi-arid region north of it live about 75,000 Goajiro Indians who provide a useful reservoir of labor.

Scattered throughout this region, and concentrated along the important rivers such as the Zulia and Catatumbo, are mixed races of Spanish, Indian and Negro. The average population density of Venezuela, however, is little more than seventeen persons to the square mile. In most sections the heat and the insect pests discourage settlement, especially of persons of white blood. The Indians who build their huts over the lake waters, do so principally to escape the insects and their attendant epidemics. The cacao and coconut plantations border the large rivers, and the three railroads that cross this region. In the hot southern part, the Indians and Negros build themselves thatched huts, and cultivate small patches of cassava and corn and a few banana trees, and concentrate on a life of leisure.

Throughout the region, the labor shortage hampers the continuance of farming in this area. The demand for labor in the oilfields is so great that many small farmers have abandoned their lands and gone to work for wages. This practice has resulted in a heavy increase in the cost of foodstuffs, and the growing need for importing more and more of the necessities of life. Since it has long been the national policy to tax all imports severely, the predicament of those who wish to live up to white standards on native income is serious.

Bordering the lake, and extending far eastward along the coast, are the temperate highlands of Venezuela, where the bulk of the population lives. These highlands are an extension of the Andes range, but they are nowhere as high as they are in other parts of South America. There are a few peaks over ten thousand feet high, and parts of the main range rise to over 15,000 feet. At the eastern end the highlands split into two ranges, with a high valley between them. There are extensive paramos, suitable for cattle grazing, at altitudes of 9,500 feet or slightly under, and a great deal of the area consists of temperate valleys. These variations in altitude and shelter, and the corresponding climates, make possible the growing of a wide range of products, from bananas to wheat.

At the western end, the lower slopes on the seaward side of the mountains are covered with dense forest which descends to merge with the tropical rain jungles of the Maracaibo Basin. In the central portion of the highland area is a great depression in which lies Lake Valencia and Valencia city. A railroad serves this entire central mountain area, tying it at one end to the port of LaGuaira and at the other end to the port of Puerto Cabello. Nine airline miles from LaGuaira is the capital, Caracas, with which it is connected by a 32-mile-long winding motor road. In recent years this road has been extended across the country to Colombia where it forms a branch of the Pan-American highway. A number of new railroads and highways have opened up additional productive lands, but in some districts transportation still depends upon the slow and inefficient mule.

While the produce of the area is of much lower dollar value than the oil of Maracaibo, it still constitutes an important source of wealth for the country and is much more important to the citizens as a whole.

Beyond the mountains to the south-east is the great interior savannah—the hundred thousand square miles of llanos that stretch from the Colombian border to the Atlantic Ocean. These plains today support several million head of cattle, but over a great deal of the area climate and soil conditions are not favorable for the production of high-grade animals. This flat land, located in a tropical climate which alternately inundates and roasts it, makes it extremely unattractive to settlers. Consequently the only people who live there are the llaneros, so that the average population density is somewhere around five persons or less to the square mile. Towns and villages are few and far between, and the main populated areas are along the Orinoco and its tributaries, and the higher ground bordering the Andes.

The largest town in Ciudad Bolívar whose population has been increased considerably since a "mountain of iron" in that neighborhood began to be exploited. Located two hundred and seventy miles from the mouths of the Orinoco, Ciudad Bolívar is the only port serving both the llanos and the Guiana highlands. Its facilities made possible not only the mining of iron ore in the El Pao area, begun in 1950, but the establishment of a steel mill near

Puerto Ordaz. As a result iron ore has become an important export from Venezuela. Also handled by this port are cattle hides, live cattle, balata, tonka beans, gold, diamonds and chicle. Imports include all kinds of cheap goods. In the dry season there is a road open to Caracas, 600 miles away, but most of the traffic goes via the river to Port of Spain, Trinidad.

The fourth natural division of the country consists of the Orinoco delta, and the Guiana highlands to the south of it. This vast area constitutes more than half of Venezuela. Part of it consists of dense tropical rain forests, out of which rise the flat tablelands, averaging eight thousand feet in altitude. Much of this area is as yet unexplored, and there are many otherwise intelligent people who cling to the notion that Sir Walter Raleigh may not have been entirely wrong, and that in those forests lies El Dorado.

Scattered through the forests, along the many streams, are the remains of early Spanish forts and attempted settlements. In almost every case the overbearing zeal of the missionaries and the depredations of the conquistadors resulted in their complete annihilation. Nevertheless, occasional placer gold mines are still worked. The rest of the exports of this region consist of forest products, such as balata, tonka, and chicle. Few permanent settlers live there and the bulk of the very thin population consists of Indians, the majority of whom have little contact with civilization and want none. The rest bring in their contributions of beans or gum as fancy dictates.

From the latest statistics available it seems that about sixty-five per cent of Venezuela's population are mestizos with a high percentage of Indian blood; only seven per cent are Indians and eight per cent Negroes. The rest are

Spanish plus fifteen thousand or so Italians, ten thousand Germans, and a lesser number of other Europeans—a total of about six millions, not counting the tribal Indians. About one fifth of the people are engaged in agricultural pursuits, and a great many more would be if it were not for the high wages paid for labor in the oil fields. Another twenty per cent of the people inhabit the coast and waterways and live principally on fish, but only ten per cent of the nation can be said to live in comfort according to modern standards.

With few flourishing industries, a great many things have to be imported besides foods, and the general condition is that dollars are comparatively cheap and local currency high. With the practically unlamented passing of dictator Gómez, the successive governments of Venezuela made some attempts to ease or correct the situation. But with the rise to power of a new military dictator in 1953, President Marcos Pérez Jiménez, the trend toward democracy came to a sudden end. His re-election for a further five-year term in 1958, however, aroused the country to such an extent that he was deposed in a popular uprising and a democratic government installed.

The attempts of previous governments to improve the lot of the people were directed along the lines of abolishing peonage, furnishing education which is compulsory in both elementary and high schools to those who can get to them, protecting labor, and improving the economic status of women. Experimental farms were established and modern farming methods abroad studied.

In common with other South American countries which recognize the need for long-range and expensive programs to spread their economy, and improve the standard of living of a 60 per cent illiterate population, the governments have initiated certain socialistic measures. These include public ownership or close regulation of industries and utilities, limitations on foreign concessions and land ownership; the abolition of church privileges, and so on. With the return to dictatorship some freedoms were lost, but the economic condition of the country as a whole remained highly prosperous.

As the world's third greatest producer of oil, Venezuela exports ninety per cent of its production. Income from this source enables the Government to carry out vast public-works programs such as bridging Lake Maracaibo to open up the Zulia region; connecting Caracas with the Caribbean by means of a tunnel; building a railway from Caracas to Puerto Cabello; building a hydro-electric plant at Caroni, and the $350,000,000 steel plant in the Guayana region which was mentioned earlier. These are a few of the undertakings already launched, and there are several others of equal importance. Only agriculture is weaker than it should be, and employment in early 1958 was 100 per cent. Economically, therefore, Venezuela is booming; and with a once-more stable and democratic government should be able to reduce its illiteracy figure substantially, while developing food production as a means of lowering living costs in this richest of South American countries.

THE GUIANAS

CHAPTER 14

THE GUIANAS: FOOTHOLDS OF EUROPE

A SLICE OF NOT PARTICULARLY SALUBRIOUS country cut out of Brazil's eastern shoulder forms the only remaining foothold of Europe in South America. This area embraces the British, Dutch, and French Guianas, the only continental colonies that have not clamored for independence.

Dutch Guiana represents a poor gamble on the part of the Netherlands who swapped it for New Amsterdam (New York) in 1667. All three of the Guianas were traded back and forth over a considerable period, when they were not being fought over by the three principal enemies of Spain during the period of her dominion over Portugal.

Early Settlements

The detailed history of the colonies is therefore somewhat confusing, but an outline of it will throw considerable light on the origins of the very mixed population that inhabit the area today. The first tentative foothold was established by the Dutch in 1616, but it remained for the English to establish a permanent settlement, complete with tobacco plantations, in 1630. The real beginnings, however, date from 1654, when Lord Willoughby, the Governor of Barbados, arrived in Surinam with a boatload of settlers among whom were a large number of Jews. Other Jews from Italy and Holland joined them, and still more migrated from Brazil when the Dutch were expelled, in that same year.

In 1655, the Jewish colonists obtained a special grant from Lord Willoughby, giving them considerable privileges in land ownership and trade—the first time in history such a thing had been done by the British Government. In 1670 the Dutch seized the colony, and Willoughby fort became Fort Zeelandia. By the Peace of Breda, 1667, Surinam was finally given to the Dutch and, as mentioned before, New York to England. A third section, now French Guiana, was awarded to France at the same time, but this did not stop both the British and the Dutch from taking it away from them on various occasions thereafter. The French regained the colony in 1676, and remained in undisturbed possession till 1809.

Meanwhile, Holland and England had resumed their periodical feuds, and Surinam flew the British flag until it was restored to the Netherlands by the Peace of Amiens in 1802. Two years later it again became a British possession, and was not relinquished until the Treaty of Paris was signed in 1814.

The French colony had also stepped aboard the merry-go-round. In 1809 an Anglo-Portuguese naval force captured the territory and handed it over to Brazil. The colony was officially returned to France by the Treaty of Paris, but the Portuguese did not leave until 1817. From then on, all was quiet on the French Guiana frontier until 1853, when gold was discovered, and border disputes arose with both Dutch Guiana and Brazil. These were settled by arbitration in 1891, 1899, and 1915.

It is unfortunate that history does not record, so far as we have been able to determine, what happened to the various colonists during those three centuries of unneighborly squabbling among the proprietary powers, but the results are there to be seen. Today British Guiana has a population of 376,000, the Dutch claim 223,000, and the French 28,500, a total of 627,500. The astonishing thing is that in spite of this comparatively small population, the total per capita trade of the Guianas exceeds that of most other countries on the continent.

This is even more surprising when the small area of productive land is considered. Out of a total of 173,141 square miles of territory, the three Guianas have under cultivation less than a quarter of a million acres! And the total occupied area is not much more, the reason being that most of the country consists of tropical rain jungles that are good for neither man nor beast. There are some grassy plains in the interior that are suitable for cattle growing. But transportation of heavy products to and from the coast is well-nigh impossible, even if there were any Guianan equivalent of the Argentine gauchos and Venezuelan llaneros to care for the stock. Consequently only the coastal strips are inhabited by the whites. The jungles are left pretty much to the bush Negroes, descendants of escaped and freed slaves who have reverted to their primitive African status. The aboriginal Indians of Arawak or Carib stock, who live along the rivers of the interior, probably do not number more than ten thousand all told.

The British Colony

Of British Guiana's 376,000 people, one fifth live in the towns. Less than five per cent of them are Europeans. During the period of original British occupation, large numbers of laborers were imported from various parts of the Empire. This accounts for the fact that there are still 180,000 East Indians in British Guiana. The balance of the population is made up of 121,000 Negroes, 41,000 of mixed blood, 10,000 Portuguese, some thousands of Chinese, and an indeterminate number of aboriginal Indians.

Sugar is the principal crop forming forty-four per cent of the country's exports, but the presence of so many Asiatics has resulted in British Guiana having become the chief rice-exporting country of South America. The East Indians also go in largely for cattle raising. The land they use is a narrow strip five or six miles wide along the coast and river banks. The excessive rain and the encroaching sea long ago made it necessary to install a tremendously expensive system of embankments, canals and sluices, to drain off the surface water and keep out the ocean. From the interior there comes a trickle of gold and diamonds, and about three thousand men are continually engaged in gathering *balatá* (an elastic gum) under government license.

Of greater potential importance, however, is the extensive mining of bauxite deposits eighty miles up the Demerara and Berbice Rivers by American and British aluminum companies. Bauxite now is the second largest export (31%). However, expansion in all lines is hampered by the lack of labor, and the climate is not calculated to attract immigrants of that class. Living conditions outside the cities are primitive, but considerable effort has been made toward combating tropical diseases and providing free education for all classes. About thirty per cent of the people are illiterate—which means that they cannot vote. Ninety-seven per cent of the school-age children are registered though they may not be within easy reach of school.

The main language is English, but many of the Asiatics still use their mother tongue in addition. They also cling to their native festivals, both Hindu and Moslem, and to the colorful clothes of the land of their origin. The men are, as a rule, good-looking and of fine physique. They wear cream-colored loin cloths, white, magenta, or saffron shirts, white or colored turbans, or perhaps a bespangled velvet cap and silver bangles. The women usually are dressed in embroidered boleros and short, white cotton shirts, with colored handkerchiefs around their heads and an assortment of gold and silver ornaments. A naturally cleanly and self-respecting people, they have an air of well-being that even drab surroundings cannot diminish.

Surinam

Although right next door to British Guiana, Surinam differs from it in many respects. For one thing, the climate is much worse because the constant trade winds that make the British colony tolerable miss Dutch Guiana altogether. This is probably one reason why there are less than five thousand Hollanders and not more than a thousand other Europeans in the country.

The population is almost as Asiatic as that of the northern colony. There are ninety-five thousand individuals originally from India and Java, and several thousand Chinese. The balance is made up of eighty thousand or so Negroes and mulattoes, plus twenty-two thousand Djukas (descendants of escaped slaves) and some thousands of other natives of mixed blood. The Javanese were originally brought into the country, after the abolition of slavery in 1863, to work as laborers on the coffee and sugar plantations. They and many of the Asiatic Indians stayed on as farm workers and numbers of them have actually become wealthy farmers and landowners, while others have made fortunes in trade.

Well over a third of the population lives in the capital city, Paramaribo, the rest of the inhabitants being distributed among half a dozen towns and populated sections along the river estuaries. Following their native custom, the Hollanders have dyked considerable portions of the coastal territory, and salvaged fertile lands for the growing of sugar, cacao, and coffee. Other important crops are oranges, bananas, and coconuts, while balata is the chief forest product. The most important export, however, is bauxite which represents eighty per cent of the export revenue, amounting to some three million tons a year. The largest mines are those owned by subsidiaries of the Aluminum Company of America. An encouraging feature of this industry is that seagoing ships can reach the mines, thanks to the navigable rivers of which there are so very few in the Guianas.

The official language of the colony is Dutch, but a great many of the people understand English. There is also a native dialect called Negro-English or talkie-talkie, which serves where the other tongues will not. The territory is run by a Governor appointed by the Queen. The legal code, the system of administration, and the general handling of public affairs, including education, is therefore substantially the same as in Holland.

French Guiana

The general physical characteristics of its neighbors extend south into French Guiana, the least developed of the three. This territory includes the large, scantily populated interior area called Inini which is administered separately.

With a population of approximately thirty-five thousand, the nine thousand acres of cultivated crops in French Guiana are needed for domestic consumption. Rum is the chief export, together with some timber and a certain amount of gold mined in a great number of scattered fields. Ordinarily the imports far exceed the exports in value.

This area was first settled in 1626, but was of little importance until penal colonies were established in 1852. These settlements covered the area around the mouth of the Maroni River, and the Îles du Salut including Devil's Island. Soon after 1940 the penal settlements were converted to refugee camps.

Today, labor in French Guiana is scarce and economic development more or less at a standstill, largely due to lack of transportation. The bush Negroes prefer a life of freedom and laziness, and the few Portuguese, Chinese, and Japanese remaining in the country are more concerned with trading than laboring. Cayenne, the capital, has a population of 13,000, but a very small proportion of the people are French. The fact that there is a substantial East Indian population is indicated by the general observance of Moslem holidays. Altogether, French Guiana promises little for the future.

So far as South America in general is concerned, these three colonies have little in common with the rest of the Continent. Luckily there also appears to be little danger of contamination from the occasional flare-ups of communism in British Guiana which the home government keeps more or less under control. Since there is also no interchange of either products or culture, the Guianas are a place apart and probably will have little influence on the future of the country as a whole. They can, therefore, for the purposes of this discussion of the South American Continent, as a political, economic, and cultural unit, be ignored.

THE RISE OF THE GREEN CONTINENT

CHAPTER 15

THE RISE OF THE GREEN CONTINENT

FROM THE FOREGOING BRIEF REVIEW of the origin and history of the South American countries it should be obvious that their similarities are greater than their differences. Underlying their unique individualities they share deep-rooted characteristics based on like origins and historic experiences. In four centuries the aboriginals and invaders have almost totally merged, and the results have been good. The combination of Latin temperament with Indian fatalism, the mixture of the volatile and the placid, the crossing of the rapier with the machete has been of inestimable benefit to both races and produced a breed that embodies the best of each. The occasional leavening with the darker strains also has benefited, in the case of Brazil in particular.

But the way has been long and hard for most of these countries. The United States of Brazil, occupying three sevenths of the whole Continent, escaped many difficulties by resisting partition into separate nations. The Spanish-American colonies, on the other hand, without exception became embroiled from time to time in fratricidal struggles for rights and territories or to satisfy the whims of dictators. And out of these minor wars developed the intense nationalistic spirit that so often set one country against its neighbor.

During the War for Independence this feeling was temporarily submerged with the countries united in a common cause. Further progress toward peace and understanding was achieved in the late nineteenth century when some of these nations finally reached a point of economic and political stability, and tensions relaxed. During this period the cultural affinities of the various regions were re-discovered and proclaimed by writers and poets who were beginning, at last, to be heard. Their outpourings transcended national loyalties and leapt international boundaries to promote a universality of spirit and extol the common ideals of the Ibero-American nations. A little later, the imperialistic ventures of the United States in Panama and elsewhere reminded them once again of the natural ties between them and their community of interest.

Since the early days of the twentieth century much has happened the world over. Vast changes have overtaken our so-called civilization—two world wars and the possibility of a third and final one have transformed nations, uniting some and dividing others, while revolutionizing industry and world commerce. Today international trade is intensely competitive; values have been distorted out of recognition, and soaring prices have wrecked hitherto stable economies. In this new world it has become obvious that John Donne's dictum that no man is an island unto himself applies equally to nations. With the whole world divided into two armed camps every country needs friends and cooperation for mere survival. And nowhere is this coming to be more clearly recognized than in South America. Today this new spirit is showing itself for all to see.

Dictatorships are vanishing to be replaced by republics inspired with democratic ideals. The days of peonage and the repression of racial and cultural minorities is coming to an end; the Ibero-American nations as a whole, at long last are awakening to their importance as an interdependent continental group ready to take their place in the world of the future that is taking shape today. That they will find such a place is inevitable; their resources are tremendous and their potential for development is almost incalculable. And they have much to offer the world in the less tangible area of a highly civilized culture.

As if recognizing these things, the less advanced of these South American countries have paid increasing attention to education, to the improvement of communications, to the extension of the franchise, and the leveling upward of opportunities. By the opening up of hitherto isolated territories education has been advanced and new industries established adding to the general prosperity in the more remote regions. But an even more significant change lies in the growth of cooperation between the nations; the apparently sudden burgeoning of an altruistic spirit in international relations that looks beyond immediate gain. In late years Brazil and Argentina and Chile in particular have taken the lead in extending aid to neighboring countries. Landlocked Bolivia and underdeveloped Paraguay have been helped immeasurably. And many of the things that all these countries have done—such as extending airlines and railways—have been of no small value to their neighbors.

But the greatest discovery of all that South America

has made is not merely the value of cooperation, but the vital necessity for each country to concentrate on the development of its own special resources instead of merely imitating its neighbors; to cultivate its own native genius instead of borrowing ideas and methods not adapted to the solution of its own specific problems.

Often it may be simpler to plant a few acres of coffee or cacao instead of undertaking a thorough and scientific survey of possibilities for something more worth while. But the country will suffer in the end. Now the trend is toward new ventures and new schemes that will best serve the country as a whole and perhaps bring prosperity to the many instead of the few.

This is the new spirit that South America is now demonstrating—the spirit that may well prove its salvation in the critical years ahead, and have a decided influence upon its sister continent to the north, and upon the world.

SELECTED BIBLIOGRAPHY

Ancient Arts of the Andes, W. C. Bennett, Museum of Modern Art, 1954
Anthropology, A. L. Kroeber, Harcourt Brace & Co., 1923
Argentina, G. Pendle, Oxford University Press, 1955
Bolivia, H. Osborne, 2nd ed., Oxford University Press, 1956
Brazil, Preston E. James, The Odyssey Press, 1946
Brazil, Henry Albert Phillips, Hastings House, 1945
Brazil, T. C. Smith, Louisiana State University Press, 1954
Brazil: People and Institutions, T. Lynn Smith, Louisiana State University Press, 1946
Caribbean, Sea of the New World, German Arciniegas, Alfred A. Knopf, 1946
Challenge of the Andes, E. G. Egeler & T. deBooy, David McKay, 1956
Chile, G. T. Butland, 3rd ed. Oxford University Press, 1956
Colombia, W. O. Galbraith, Royal Institute of International Affairs, 1953
Concerning Latin American Culture, Columbia University Press, 1944
Economic Geography of South America, Whitbeck & Williams, McGraw Hill Book Co., 1940

Ecuador, Arturo Eichler, Heinemann, 1955

Good Neighbors, Hubert Herring, Yale University Press, 1944

Industry in Latin America, George Wythe, Columbia University Press, 1945

Kunst im Reiche du Inka, H. U. Doering, Tübingen, 1952

Latin America in Maps, A. Curtis Wilgus, Barnes & Noble, 1943

Latin American Civilization, Bailey W. Diffie, Stackpole Sons, 1945

Paraguay, P. Raine, Scarecrow, 1956

Peruvian Economy, Pan-American, 1950

South America, Clarence F. Jones, Henry Holt & Co., 1942

South American Handbook, Edited: Howell Davies, Trade & Travel Publications, London, 1943

South American Handbook, Wilson, 1955

South American Primer, Katherine Carr Rodell, Reynal & Hitchcock, 1941

U. S. and South America, A. P. Whitaker, Harvard University Press, 1956

Uruguay, H. Fitzgibbon, Rutgers University Press, 1954

Venezuela, Business & Finance, R. Lugardo, Prentice-Hall, 1957

INDEX

Illustrations are indicated by plate numbers in italics

B

C

G

H

I

N

O

P

Q

R

U

V

W

Y

Z

1
2
3
4
5
6
7
8
9
10
11
12
13
14
15
16
17
18
19
20
21
22
23
24
25
26
27
28
29
30
31
32
33
34
35
36
37
38
39
40
41
42
43
44
45
46
47
48
49
50
51
52
53
54
55
56
57
58
59
60
61